D0435925

◆ ❖ ◆

"I think Shaun's new book is what you'd expect to see from a man like him. He is a great runner on the field and well-grounded in family and spirituality off it. I'd recommend this book to anyone who is interested in good guys finishing first on the field and in life."

—**Barry Sanders,**
Pro Football Hall of Fame/Class of 2004

"In his new book, Shaun Alexander shows people of all ages and races that we are all God's children. He is a living example of persistence overcoming resistance!"

—**Salome Thomas-EL,**
educator, bestselling author of *I Choose to Stay* and *The Immortality of Influence*

"Shaun shines even brighter as a Christian than as the 2005 Most Valuable Player in the NFL. He is one of God's choicest servants, the real deal."

—**Wayne Atcheson,**
Director, Billy Graham Library; former national staff member of the Fellowship of Christian Athletes; author, *Faith of the Crimson Tide*

"Shaun...is inspiring young men to grow into the leaders and strong family men God has destined them to be."

—**Casey Treat,**
Senior Pastor, Christian Faith Center, Seattle, Washington

◆ ❖ ◆

TOUCHDOWN ALEXANDER

SHAUN ALEXANDER
with CECIL MURPHEY

HARVEST HOUSE PUBLISHERS

EUGENE, OREGON

Shaun Alexander is published in association with the agency of SFX Football, 222 S. Central Ave., Suite 108, St. Louis, MO 63105.

Cecil Murphey is published in association with the literary agency of The Knight Agency, 570 East Ave., Madison, GA 30650.

Cover by Koechel Peterson & Associates, Inc., Minneapolis, Minnesota

Front and back cover photos © Corky Trewin/Seattle Seahawks; Author photo on book jacket © Justin Kercher/ JAK Studios

Also available as an audiobook, with a bonus exclusive interview with Shaun and former NFL quarterback Rodney Peete and play-by-play audio of some of Shaun's greatest moments with the Seattle Seahawks.

TOUCHDOWN ALEXANDER
Copyright © 2006 by Shaun Alexander
Published by Harvest House Publishers
Eugene, Oregon 97402
www.harvesthousepublishers.com

Library of Congress Cataloging-in-Publication Data
Alexander, Shaun.
Touchdown Alexander / Shaun Alexander with Cecil Murphey.
p. cm.
ISBN-13: 978-0-7369-1937-1 (hardcover)
ISBN-10: 0-7369-1937-6
Product # 6919371
1. Alexander, Shaun. 2. Running backs (Football)—United States—Biography. I. Murphey, Cecil B. II. Title.
GV939.A48A3 2006
796.332092—dc22
[B]
2006011245

Printed in the United States of America

06 07 08 09 10 11 12 13 14 / LB-CF / 10 9 8 7 6 5 4 3 2 1

To my wife, Valerie,
and our two baby girls, Heaven and Trinity.

Thanks for showing me that God does bless His obedient child.

Acknowledgments

Carol Alexander, Momma—thanks for showing me how to love unconditionally, and teaching me the value of character and discipline.

Durran Alexander—thanks for bringing a spirit of excellence and joy to my life.

Curtis Alexander, Dad—thanks for showing me it is okay to apologize and forgive.

To my family, "The Jacksons"—thank you for love, support, and honesty as I journeyed from boy to man.

Owen Hauck and the Boone County Rebels—thanks for leadership, the friendships, the great memories; and showing me the value of a great team.

The University of Alabama—thanks for helping me become a champion on and off the field…Roll, Tide!!!

The Seattle Seahawks—thanks for coming through when it counted.

Christian Faith Center, my home church—thanks for reminding me that Jesus wants the best for my life.

To my Pauls, Barnabases, and Timothys—thanks for being a part of my life, whether you are one of my teachers, encouragers, or students.

CONTENTS

A WORD FROM
COACH GENE STALLINGS

During my years as head coach of the Crimson Tide, I saw many players with great talent. Shaun Alexander was one of them, one of the best. I also saw many players who were willing to work hard to develop their talent. Shaun did this as well.

There were not many, though, with Shaun's big, generous heart. Sure, he needed some training and coaching in the best way to live out his generosity, but he's always found himself good mentors and advisors who could help him do the right thing. I am especially proud that he hasn't let the fame and wealth of professional football go to his head. Instead, he's put his time and money into helping boys in need become men—real men who can be dads and leaders. That's something that's especially near to my heart.

I've had the privilege of coaching lots of players who went on and had outstanding careers in the NFL, but the only player, to my knowledge, that gave something back to the University of Alabama was Shaun Alexander. He gave a sizeable check to the Rise Program—a program on the Alabama campus where mentally challenged youngsters go to early intervention training for five weeks to five years. Ninety-five percent of these children mainstream into kindergarten, and if it weren't for the generosity of people like Shaun and others, this program would not be possible.

I asked Shaun why he did it, and he simply said, "It's the right thing to do."

◆ ❖ ◆

Shaun has lived what he calls a "blessed life." He gives God credit for this—which is right—but I have to point out the fact that Shaun has taken every blessing, turned it around, and passed it on to others. Because of that, his playing years are just the beginning. He's going to keep moving forward into his *best* years.

In the following pages you'll meet an outstanding football player who's also grown into a great husband, father, and man. God bless you, Shaun, and keep passing on the blessing to others.

Gene Stallings

Gene Stallings
Head Coach, Alabama Crimson Tide, 1990–1996

THINK BIG, BELIEVE BIG

My name is Shaun Alexander, and I'm a running back for the Seattle Seahawks football team.

That's what I *do*, but that's not who I *am*. Football is something I'm good at, but it isn't my total life. I'm also a husband, a father, and a Christian man. I'm a mentor to younger men as well, because they are our future.

My story is not in any way a tragic one. I don't have a great traumatic incident in my past that caused me to turn to God. To tell you the truth, my life has been blessed with a great deal of happiness and success.

At times, I've felt a little bad about that. Most of the time, though, I just end up reminding myself that I am who I am because I had a wise mother, who not only took me to church and taught me about Jesus' love but who has lived the life she taught me to live.

I think one of the entries in my journal from when I was feeling down sums it up for me: "My success and values haven't come from anguished trials. My success and values have come from God, and I must honor God—not the trial."

So with such a blessed life, without a lot of tragedy—why am I writing my story now? There are several reasons, and here are some of the most important:

- I want my story to serve as an example because, in a way, my success is more about the goodness of God than it is about anything I've done to warrant praise.

- I want to show people—especially young people—that success is closer than they may think. And I want people to realize that God is the key to success.

- I want to encourage people to set goals for their lives—the higher the better. If we think big and believe big, we'll *act* big and move in big ways. As a result, we'll enjoy life in a big way.

Life really *is* to enjoy—to have fun and laugh a lot. If we're not enjoying our life, something isn't right. Forget your adverse circumstances. God is greater than what's going on around you. Lean on Him. You *will* make it through.

TOUCHDOWN
ALEXANDER

Chapter 1

MY BEGINNINGS

To understand who I've become, you should know a few things about where I've come from, and you need to meet some of the family and friends who helped me grow up thinking big and believing big.

The best way is to start with my birth. I was born to Curtis and Carol Alexander on August 30, 1977, in Florence, Kentucky. (Florence is a town in Boone County, just across the Ohio River from Cincinnati.) That was about one year after my brother, Durran, was born. Aside from being near in age, Durran and I have always been close. Even today, I don't make many moves until I bounce them off my brother.

Our family lived in a two-bedroom apartment at the Shenandoah Apartments on Shenandoah Drive in Florence. Yes, it was small...but I don't remember it that way. For me, that apartment and the bedroom I shared with my brother seem more like a mansion in my memories. Maybe that's because our mom made us feel like we had everything we needed. We knew we weren't rich, but we never felt like we were poor.

Durran and I learned to lean on each other at an early age. Our parents separated when I was 11, and he and I stayed with our mom. In some ways Durran's been my father figure, and he's always been more mature than me.

Another reason I felt we had such a great home is that Mom made all my friends feel welcome there. They loved to spend the night with us.

Ironically, most of those friends lived in houses (and some of them were huge), not apartments.

During those growing-up years, there were six guys I always hung with. The two youngest were my cousin, Ben Brown, and Jason List, who lived up the street. They were two grades below me. Then there were my four best friends: Ray Arnold, Brian Maney, Josh Hays, and Scott Woodall. We became the kind of friends that—though all extremely different from each other—stuck together through the years. And we're still close today.

While Mom and Dad were married, we also had a lot of contact with my three older half-brothers and four half-sisters from my dad's previous marriage. They grew up in Cincinnati, and although they never lived with us, we still spent a lot of time together.

> **I became a Christian at a young age, and that decision had a powerful influence on me in my teen years and gave me the ethical principles on which to operate.**

Of my three half-brothers—Donte, Ronnie, and Tony—I always felt closest to Ronnie, my middle half-brother. He joined the army as soon as he finished high school. I was still in grade school, but Ronnie used to phone me regularly, and that meant a lot to me. It thrilled me to have him call from various places in the United States and overseas. One time he called from France, and another time from his base in Germany. He never wanted anything except to say hello, ask how I was doing, and let me know he loved me.

Donte, the oldest of the five of us Alexander boys, is bright, works hard, and constantly pushes himself to do big things in the business world. And Tony is the stereotypical middle child. People always seemed to pay more attention to his older or younger brothers. Tony is also the quietest and most private of the five of us. In his school days, he was a good football player. After I started to excel in the game, I'd tease him and say, "Tony, you're the second-best athlete in the family."

"And who's the first?" he'd ask.

"You're lookin' at him!" I'd respond, and we'd both laugh.

When I was growing up, my half-brothers—especially Tony—seemed to think Dad spent a lot of time with me. Maybe that was because Dad lived with us until he and Mom split up. Maybe it was because Dad would try to come to all my games when I was in high school. To tell the truth, aside from coming to see me play, Dad didn't really spend much time with me or with Durran either—or at least not as much time as we wanted. But Tony's feelings made him chalk up my success on the football field to Dad's presence. He used to say, "Shaun, Dad put you in your shoes."

I think he knows better now, and I certainly do. Dad wasn't the one who put me in my shoes. Instead, I point to two things that carried me forward. First, I became a Christian at a young age, and that decision had a powerful influence on me in my teen years and gave me the ethical principles on which to operate. Second, I learned early that it takes self-discipline to be successful. That firm ethical base and my commitment to self-discipline pushed me forward.

My relationship with my dad did have some major influences on my life, as you'll read about later. In fact, family played a large part in my early years. One of my favorite memories of childhood has to do with our family Christmases. We usually celebrated at the home of my mother's parents. And no matter who you were—if you were *there,* you got a present. Everybody received a present—I mean *everybody.*

Several of my friends didn't have big families, so they loved to go with us to my grandparents' to celebrate the holiday. Something was going on the whole time we were there. My friends also knew they'd eat the best food in the world. Afterward, they'd rave about their time with us and say they felt loved at Grandma's house. Although we were only kids and couldn't really describe it, we could all sense the warmth there.

When we'd drive to our grandparents' house, it seemed like our car was filled with gifts to give away. And when we arrived, the huge Christmas tree would be surrounded by presents. Toys, clothes, money—all sorts of fun gifts, everywhere. Early Christmas morning we'd open our gifts…but first we'd sing "Must Be Santa," a song we learned when we were in elementary school.

We had a limitless number of verses, and Durran would sing them while the rest of us joined him in the chorus. The only part I got to sing by myself (ripping as if I stood on the stage of the Apollo Theater) was the names of the reindeer.

And as soon as we finished, we'd start the song again.

After that, we received and opened our gifts. My mother had six sisters and one brother, so we always had a big gathering, what with all the cousins and friends who'd come along. Mom was next to the oldest in her family, but she usually played the role of the oldest because her older sister, Aunt Gwen, had married a military man and they lived in New Mexico.

> I remember that no one ever left the house without a gift...I thought it was the coolest thing in the world that my grandparents always had extra gifts to give away to unexpected guests.

No one was allowed to open anything until all the gifts had been passed out. After everyone had their gifts we'd unwrap them, one at a time, and hold them up. We'd show each other what we'd received. That was a special time. Someone would cry out, "How did you know that's what I wanted!" Another person would whisper, "You gave me my favorite gift."

Christmas was an all-day affair at Grandma's house. No one knew when it would end—and it usually went on long into the night.

Of course, there were football games on TV, but we didn't turn on the set. Instead, we just sat around and visited—talking about what was going on in our lives. After everyone had a chance to talk, we had prayer, and then we'd eat.

Mostly I remember that no one ever left the house without a gift. Even when friends decided to come at the last minute, they would still leave with presents. That always amazed me because it seemed that no matter who they were, they received a new sweatshirt or a toy or something else they didn't expect. I thought it was the coolest thing in the world that my grandparents always had extra gifts to give away to unexpected guests.

Perhaps it all doesn't sound exciting, but it was more than the words, the music, or the gift-giving. It was togetherness with one grandma, one grandpa, and a dozen or so aunts and uncles, along with 30 or 40 cousins and friends. I grew up with that sense of being a family and loving one another. For me, Christmas wasn't about presents, it was about family—our large and loving family.

◆ ❖ ◆

That sense of being part of a loving family worked itself out in the way I felt about Durran. He's the coolest brother anyone could have. As I look back on our childhood (and this is just as true today), I remember he was good at everything, and I always wanted to be exactly like him. For instance, when he started to play sports, *I* started to play sports. He set the pattern for me.

All through school, I remained "Durran's younger brother." I suppose I could have responded by becoming the class clown or the dumb kid—I know that happens—but I really wanted to be like Durran, and I tried hard to emulate him. Though I never did feel I was as good at anything as he was, I never stopped trying. He made straight A's in his classes, and although I didn't tie his record, I did get close.

Because Durran was a year ahead of me, I was constantly reminded that I didn't measure up to him. I didn't resent him for this. Yet I wished I had been smarter and had been able to pull better grades than he had…but I never could do it.

Here's a typical example of the sort of thing that would happen. On my first morning in class one year, the teacher, Mrs. Rankin, arranged us alphabetically and called out our names. She pointed to the first row, first seat, and called out, "Shaun Alexander."

When I sat down, she said, "Oh, Shaun—you must be Durran's brother."

"Yes, ma'am," I said.

"I know I'm going to enjoy having you," she said, beaming. "I had a wonderful time teaching Durran last year." Mrs. Rankin went on to say what an excellent student my brother had been. I had heard that same statement every year on the first day of school from some teacher who already had taught him the year before. And it was true—Durran *was* an amazing student and one of the brightest kids in school.

As soon as Mrs. Rankin finished praising him, she paused and looked at me as if she expected me to say something. I decided to do something to change the mood, so without waiting for her permission, I told a joke. Everyone in the class laughed.

Mrs. Rankin laughed as hard as the rest of them.

When the class began to quiet down, she said, "That was funny, Shaun. Durran told us that one last year, and it's still funny."

◆ ❖ ◆

It's easy to think I might have lived my whole life as just "Durran's little brother." But whenever I'd start to feel that was true, I'd think of what Mrs. Walton told me when I was in sixth grade.

Mrs. Walton was our science teacher. As usual, my brother had been in her class the year before. Something happened early in the year—I don't remember exactly what—but I think it had to do with the grade I'd received on a test. I had tried hard. My grade wasn't very good, however. I didn't fail, but I knew it was nothing close to what Durran had made.

When Mrs. Walton returned our test papers, I stared at my grade. My eyes began to fill with tears, and I couldn't hold them back. I was really discouraged, and Mrs. Walton could tell. She didn't say anything right then, but as soon as the class ended, she pulled me aside.

"Shaun, you'll do better on the next test," she told me.

I shook my head. "You want me to be just like Durran."

She gazed into my eyes and said softly, "No, you don't have to be like Durran. You just have to be the best Shaun the world's ever seen."

Those words clicked inside my head.

No one had ever told me I had to be like Durran—that was something *I* had decided. Maybe because I loved and admired my older brother, I felt I had to duplicate everything he did. I assumed everyone expected me to compete with whatever he did. But from that day on, I no longer had to be the smartest kid, the most popular, or the most charming. I never stopped loving and admiring Durran, and I never stopped trying to be good in school, but that day I learned I didn't have to be like him or to be as good as he was.

I just needed to be the best Shaun I could be—the best Shaun the world has ever seen.

That's been my goal ever since.

Chapter 2

I'M A BELIEVER

can't recall a Sunday in my childhood when we weren't at St. Stephen's Missionary Baptist Church in the Walnut Hills section of Cincinnati.

I loved the music at St. Stephen's. The singing was fully alive. To this day I carry warm memories of being there, and inside my head I can hear some of the songs we sang.

Even as a boy, when I listened to the choir sing, I *knew* they were connecting with God. I don't remember all the adults in the choir, but I do remember Sister Maxine. She had an unbelievable, soul-piercing voice. I felt good just being there and listening.

Every Sunday morning I wanted to get to church on time so I could hear the choir and sing with the congregation. I have to admit, though, that the preaching didn't do much for me. More than anything else, I went for the music.

But then, when I was about ten years old and in fourth grade, something important happened—something that would change the course of my life. That's when I finally started to pay attention to what Floyd Brown, our pastor, was saying.

I vividly remember it. It was Easter Sunday, 1987. I gazed up at the choir. Their shining faces and joyful voices were better than any rock group I'd seen on TV. I was totally immersed in the music. One man near us was clapping his hands and jumping up and down—he too was totally lost in the music. To my left, a woman ran up and down the aisle, shouting and praising God. I thought she was probably a little crazy, but there was no mistaking the joy on her face.

A woman near me rocked back and forth in her seat as she sang. Then she stopped and cried out, "Thank you, Jesus!" By then, the choir members had their hands raised and were singing joyful praises.

I leaned over and whispered to my mother, "What's going on?"

"That's their way of responding to God," Mom said. Very quietly, she explained, "Shaun, some of these people have big problems—so big they don't know if they'll come out of them. But they will. Others are in the middle of trials, and life is hard for them right now—very hard." She pointed to one friend. "That lady has been having a bad week, and she has many burdens. When she comes to church, she can let go of them all and know that God will bless her. Some others are saying, 'God, I believe in You.' Others are saying, 'With Your help, God, I'm going to make it through another week.'"

> I silently prayed my first significant prayer: "God, I don't know much, but I do know how to be obedient."

"That's cool," I said.

By then, Mom's arm was around my shoulder. She talked to me about how much Jesus Christ loves each one of us. "Jesus can pull us out of any trials—no matter how big they are," she told me.

I listened to her—and I kept watching everyone. Some of them did act strangely, but now I understood—they were responding to God's love in their own way.

Finally I turned and said, "Momma, I need to know this Jesus."

Patiently, she explained to me that Jesus loves me, had died to take away my sins, and wants me to love Him in return. She spoke in such simple terms that I didn't have trouble understanding. Although that wasn't the first time I had heard the good news about Jesus Christ, it was the first time the words got through to me. Momma then explained that if I truly loved Jesus, I would be obedient to Him in every way.

All the messages I had heard for the ten years I'd been going to church and Sunday school fell into place that day. It all made sense. So as I listened, I silently prayed my first significant prayer: "God, I don't know much, but I do know how to be obedient."

At the end of the service that Easter Sunday, Pastor Brown looked out at us and asked, "Do any of you want to give your life to Christ? Does anybody want to join the church?"

I turned to Mom and asked, "Can I go?"

She nodded.

I walked up to the front, and Pastor Brown welcomed me and prayed for me. The next Sunday, I was baptized and joined the church.

Very early I learned that we make choices. We can make choices that enable us to live blessed lives on earth and eventually lead us to heaven. We have to choose which path we will follow—we have to choose to love, to forgive, and to enjoy being alive. And we show how we've decided by the way we live. We practice obedience.

I've also learned that Jesus wants to love us and help us to make those right choices. I can't say I've always made the best ones, but I've made many good ones since the day I decided to follow Jesus Christ. And the result of that obedience has been blessing in my life.

That decision to follow Jesus Christ was just the beginning. From that day on, I tried to live like a Christian in every area of my life. And when I entered high school, I started to think even more seriously about my faith.

As I looked around, I saw how some people compared themselves to others, and I decided that was a foolish thing to do. Or I noticed they made bad choices because they felt it brought acceptance from their peers. Some of my classmates drank and others were involved in sex because that's what they saw their friends do.

That kind of behavior didn't make sense to me. I decided that I had to recognize right from wrong for myself and then do the right thing just because it was the right thing—even if it wasn't the popular thing. I didn't want to compare myself to others or think I was better than someone else. I just wanted to be a person who followed his heart and his convictions. I wanted to be the best Shaun I could be.

Even when my friends didn't do what I thought was the right thing, that didn't excuse *me* from needing to make good choices. I just didn't get into that comparison game or start judging others by how they behaved. Several people I knew were like the guy who says, "You're shooting heroin, and that's bad. I may smoke a little weed now and then, but at least I don't do heroin." He's saying he's better because his habit isn't as bad as the other, so that makes him a better person. Even as a teenager, I realized that those who compare themselves like that are off the track as much as the people they criticize or judge.

For me, right and wrong have always been pretty simple. Either something is good or it isn't. And I believe God has blessed me with the ability to pay attention to what is right and stay away from what is wrong. That has helped me avoid a lot of problems in life.

For example, ever since high school, people have offered me alcohol or wanted me to smoke weed with them. I've always refused. Back then, I didn't think of the consequences, only that I just didn't feel right about doing either one. I've never been drunk or high, and I don't feel I've missed anything by living sober. Now that I'm older, I realize the effects of such things on people. Drugs and alcohol can destroy a life. I knew I didn't want them to destroy mine. So, for me, the principle has been very simple: If it doesn't feel right to do—even though I can't explain the reason—I don't do it.

Take the matter of sex—which I write more about later. I knew it was wrong to have sex outside of marriage. Some of my friends—both Christian and non-Christian—went ahead and became sexually active in their teens, but I couldn't believe it was right. And later I learned the teachings of the Bible about sexual immorality and realized I was right to not get caught up in that trap. As a result, I abstained from sex until I married.

◆ ❖ ◆

A lot of my friends liked to party. "Let's hit the clubs," they'd say. "Let's party." I was often the ringleader who got them to the club, but I knew where to draw the line. But some of them would start to drink and wouldn't stop until they were drunk.

When I would go to the clubs with them, I went because I wanted to be around people I liked. I enjoyed talking, laughing, and hanging with my friends. Just being around them kept me entertained all night. When it was time to leave, I left. Sometimes I had to leave early because things had gotten out of hand or I felt I needed to get away from situations I knew I wasn't supposed to get into. I never felt I had to stay just because some of my friends did.

One day, though, I asked myself if I was doing the right thing by encouraging my friends to party—friends who obviously couldn't control themselves. I started to realize I had been wrong to take people with me who couldn't handle the temptations around them.

One big event especially convinced me of this.

During my senior year, we finally came to that great moment many of us had looked forward to: spring break.

A bunch of us guys decided to go to Panama City, Florida—the popular meeting place for most of the schools on the Eastern Seaboard.

My mom had one big question: "Who's going with you?"

I told her that it would be me, Brian, Ray, and another friend, Steve Beegle.

She noted that Ray and Steve knew how to drive—and I didn't. So she said, "Shaun, I think you need to learn to drive too."

That was a great idea. And I knew what she was really thinking: *You need to learn how to drive so you can take over in case the others get drunk.*

So by the time spring break rolled around, I had my license, and off the four of us went.

All of us had heard stories about the drinking and wild parties, so on the drive south I said to the others, "You know, we're going to see a lot of drinking. So what are we going to do?"

"I'm not going to drink," Brian said.

"Cool—then I won't either," I said—even though I was never interested in drinking anyway, no matter how many times I was around it.

"I'm not going to drink either," Ray added.

Steve agreed. No drinking.

It was about three in the morning when we checked into a motel near the beach. We slept a few hours and then headed out to the beach to see all the honeys. We also saw a lot of our friends from Boone County and other places. It seemed as if the whole country was there.

That afternoon we ate, strolled around, and saw people. Around sunset, somehow we lost Ray. We looked around but never could find him—not on the beach, not in our room…he just wasn't around.

We went out to eat some dinner and then decided to look for him again. As we began walking toward one of the hotels where we'd heard there was a party going on—it was close to midnight by then—we caught sight of Ray about 20 feet ahead.

"Man, what have you been doing?" I asked.

"I was just over here chilling," he slurred.

I stared at him and repeated my question. "What have you been doing?"

"Man, I'm messed up," he mumbled. "I'm drunk."

"Yeah, we can tell," I replied.

He felt humiliated, not so much because he was drunk, but because he had broken his word.

"I'm really messed up," he repeated. "I've been drinking all day."

We all walked back to the hotel room, put Ray to bed, and then turned in ourselves.

Early the next morning the phone rang. I knew it was my mom.

"You guys doing good?" she asked. "How was ya'll's first night?"

"We're doing fine," I said.

"Ray didn't have too much to drink, did he?"

I started laughing. "Mama, we made a pact we're not going to drink, so we're all just over here chilling."

"Really?" she said. "So Ray didn't drink last night?"

I didn't answer the question and changed the subject. It wouldn't have done any good to lie anyway. Mom would figure that out too.

We talked a few more minutes before I hung up the phone. I smiled as I thought of Mom's incredible sense of always knowing what everybody was doing. I never did find out how she knew Ray had been drinking—but we didn't fool her. She knew.

Mom really did care about what happened to my friends as well as me. I wanted to honor her for that care and follow her great example. So I made a decision: I would never take my friends to clubs again. I would not encourage them to put themselves into situations where they'd end up getting into trouble.

When you know what's right and wrong, all you have to do is make that decision to do right, avoid wrong—and follow through.

Here's an example of how that worked out one time.

One night I borrowed my mother's car, and several of us went to a friend's apartment to play cards. I saw a lot of drinking and drug-taking going on.

As the evening wore on, people kept coming and going from the apartment, and I felt more and more uncomfortable. It wasn't long before things were getting out of hand and I decided I'd better make an exit.

"We gotta get out of here, *now!*" I said to a couple of my friends. I grabbed them and we left.

We went out to the car and just as we started to drive away, a police car came up behind us and pulled us over. The officer got out, came up to my window, and then looked me over.

"Aren't you Shaun Alexander?" he asked.

"Yes, sir," I said.

"Did you come out of this apartment right here?"

"Yes, sir, I did," I replied.

"Have you been drinking?" he asked.

"Sir, I don't drink," I told him.

"I don't know," he said slowly. "You sure *smell* like it."

I laughed and said, "No, I really don't drink."

He paused a moment. "Okay, I believe you," he said. "But you need to watch the company you keep. We've been keeping an eye on that apartment for quite a while."

That was all the warning I needed.

I thanked him and drove away. Whether the police knew I was in there and were trying to protect their homegrown high school football hero, I don't know. I just know I could have been a statistic that night—but I thank God I wasn't.

◆ ❖ ◆

Somebody once asked me if I had ever been caught sneaking out to go to a party scene. Here's my only story about something that was bad—and could have been worse.

We had finished my junior football season, and I wanted to go to a party at my teammate Jason Smith's farmhouse. "Chainsaw," as we called him, was throwing a field party on some land about half an hour's drive from the city. When I first mentioned it, my mom said she didn't feel good about my going, so I cooked up a scheme to get out there. It was supposed to be the party of the year, and I didn't want to miss it.

So I told my mom I would spend the night at Jason's house, knowing she would think I meant Jason List—my friend who lived up the street. But I planned to go to Jason Smith's place. I reasoned I hadn't lied to her—although of course I had.

I walked to Jason List's house, and my friend Brandi met me there and drove me to Chainsaw's party. It started out fine, and I was having a lot of fun. However, about midnight, I wasn't feeling well and decided I should go home.

I left the party with some friends, who dropped me off at our family's apartment. But just before I went inside, I remembered I was supposed to be at Jason List's house. So I walked back there. In my letterman jacket I usually carried golf balls, and I pulled out a couple of them and threw them at Jason's window to get his attention. He woke up, looked out, waved, and came down and opened the front door. I walked inside and said, "Jason, I'm sick." I then went into the basement and fell asleep on the couch.

Mom had always said we could spend the night away from home, but she had set rules for us to follow. For example, we couldn't spend the night without asking about it a day in advance. We could never "impulse spend the night," is the way she said it. And if we spent the night somewhere, we had to call her first thing the next morning to tell her what we planned to do that day.

That night I must have caught a virus because I was sick—really sick. I threw up several times, staggered back to the couch each time, and kept going back to sleep.

The next morning I didn't call home, and Mom was worried. When she called Jason List's house, his mother said I wasn't there, because she didn't know I was asleep in the basement. I guess Jason had forgotten to tell her.

Mom naturally thought I had lied about staying there. She kept calling around trying to find me and getting more and more worried—and upset—with each phone call.

I never did learn who did it, but someone squealed about my going to Chainsaw's party and told Mom the truth about everything I had done the night before.

When I finally came awake, it was one-thirty in the afternoon. Immediately I called home. I tried to be smooth. I told Mom I had slept too late and assumed she would understand. I had it all planned inside my head what I would say.

But it didn't go that way.

"Didn't I say I had something to do today?" she reminded me as soon as she heard my voice.

"Yes, Mom," I replied, "but I wasn't feeling good, so I slept in."

"No, that's not true," she said. "Shaun, I know why you slept in. And you need to get home. *Right now!*"

That walk only took about five minutes, but it seemed like it took five hours. I felt as if vultures were circling around me the whole time. I don't remember exactly what Momma said, but it was something about trust and honoring someone—and the importance of good character.

I hung my head as she talked. She was right—and I promised myself I would never do that again. And I didn't. Never again did I sneak out to a party or try to tell a half-lie to my mother.

I knew I had good character. And I liked having an open, trusting relationship with my mother. I never wanted her to doubt me again.

That experience helped me to realize something else: If I did something wrong, not only did I hurt myself, but I dishonored Mom. I truly wanted to honor her in everything I did.

Looking back, it was to my advantage to have a mother like that. She was the queen of discipline. She kept things very strict in our home. All my friends knew that too, because if they were in our house, Mom disciplined them as well. But Mom balanced her discipline with love. One way she did this was when she told my brother, my friends, or me—which she did often—"No matter what trouble you get into, I'll get you out of that trouble—the first time. After that, you're on your own."

I laughed just about every time she said that. I laughed, but I knew she was serious. So did my friends. We all knew it was because she was also serious about loving us and wanting us to make good decisions—and be obedient.

"I don't know much, but I do know how to be obedient."

Today, 20 years after I prayed with my mom on that Easter Sunday, I still say those same words to myself almost every day. That simple sentence has become the spiritual slogan for my life. I believe a major reason I am who I am today is that I remember those words, try to live by them, and never want to forget them.

Chapter 3

FOOTBALL BEGINS

When I was in second grade, my brother Durran and our friend Ray Arnold announced one day they were going to join the local peewee football team. They talked about becoming big sports stars and about how much fun it would be. They asked me to play, but I wasn't interested.

I was the kind of kid who didn't mind sitting in the house and watching TV. Or sometimes I liked to just sit and daydream about my future. In my thoughts, I was always the boss—very successful, of course—I wore fine suits and was an excellent leader of the people who worked for me. I told Durran and my friends about what I imagined. They laughed, but I believed in my dreams.

A few days after their announcement, Durran and Ray raced enthusiastically into our apartment with the news: "We just had our first practice!"

"We exercised and did a whole bunch of football drills," Durran said. He started to explain the plays and repeat how much fun they had. I could *feel* their enthusiasm.

"Shaun, you *have* to come," Ray interrupted. "Tomorrow we get pads!"

"No, I don't like running," I said. "Ya'll go ahead. Tell me about it tomorrow."

The next day, they came back after practice even *more* excited.

"We got *hit* today!" Ray shouted.

They told me everything that had happened. Every few minutes one of them would pause and say, "Shaun, you *gotta* join us!"

"Are ya'll still doing all that running?" I asked.

"Yes, and it's fun!" Ray said.

"I'm not interested," I replied.

At the end of the first week of practice, Durran and Ray raced over to the apartment to relive their fun time for me again. I tried to resist, but they had begun to wear me down. By the beginning of the second week, I gave in and joined them on the team.

To my surprise, I actually *liked* playing football.

But there was something about it I liked even better. And that was *after* the Saturday game—when Durran and I would invite our teammates to our apartment for pizza, Doritos, and ice cream. Usually, a couple guys from our team would end up spending the night. It was great fun.

> That was my start in playing football—when I was still more interested in the pizza and fun with friends than in the game itself.

Each time, Mom's conditions were the same: "You boys can eat all the pizza, chips, and ice cream you want. You can play games and have fun tonight, but everyone gets up Sunday morning and goes to church."

No one ever argued over that arrangement. I thought that was the greatest trade in the world. So I invited my friends over almost every Saturday night. I'd have two, three, or sometimes four kids with me, and we'd go to church together the next day. Since we had only a two-bedroom apartment it was amazing we could have so many people spend the night...but we did.

Looking back, I'm convinced that Mom's great attitude shaped my desire to invite people to church all the time. After the Saturday night games and the goodies that followed, my friends would often say, "Shaun, you've got the best mom in the world."

That was something I already knew.

And that was my start in playing football—when I was still more interested in the pizza and fun with friends than in the game itself.

In third grade, I played defense. In fourth grade, the coach made me the kick returner. The first game of the season, the opening kickoff came right to me. I caught the ball and ran it back for a touchdown. A few minutes later, the other team scored, and they kicked off to me again. I caught the ball another time and ran it back for a second touchdown.

The other team scored again and then again…and again. They beat us 38–12.

Our team walked slowly off the field, dejected. But it amazed me that in spite of our loss, people were excited about how I'd played. My mom, spectators—even players from the other team—raved about what I had done. "You made *two* touchdowns, Shaun! That's awesome!" They made it sound like we'd won the game. I was amazed at the attention I received just from scoring those two times.

Afterward I asked Durran, "What position scores the most touchdowns?"

"Probably the running back," he said.

I smiled.

That day a running back was born.

The coach I most remember from those days was Tony Roedig. I had him in sixth grade. He was a yeller and was constantly screaming at me, "Stiff arm!" Coach Roedig believed the stiff arm was the answer for anyone who tried to tackle me. Tony was tough and had eyes of fire that could intimidate anybody and everybody. We were all a little afraid of him. But that fear caused us to play well so we wouldn't have to mess with his yelling at us. Because of his motivation, we lost only three games in two years.

It was also in sixth grade I realized I was really good at football. That's when it started to seem easy to score touchdowns. That's also when I figured out I could do something not everybody else could do.

In seventh grade, when I played under Coach Pollack, and in eighth grade, I was on really good teams. Though we played against stronger opponents, making touchdowns still seemed easy. In ninth grade, I played freshman football under Coach Fulmer. He was my health teacher and a fun coach. He believed in a passing offense. So in addition to carrying the ball for yardage, I learned to catch passes and push for more yards that way. That year our team lost about as many games as we won, but I still had a good time. Even in the games we lost, I managed to score a lot of touchdowns.

From my sophomore year through my senior year at Boone County High School, we trained with Dave Guidugli, one of the history teachers, who we called the "Guru of Fitness." He was different from the other coaches I'd had. Coach Guidugli was a wild man. I think that's what impressed me. He trained high school, college, and pro athletes to get stronger and faster.

"I train only the best," he repeated frequently, "and I'm around only the best." He used to tell us stories about when he was young and foolish and got into fights. "There's nothing wrong with standing up for what you believe," he said, "but if you're going to stand up, then *stand up.*"

Dave set up all our lifting and running programs and even put us on a boxing team. Not only was he a great coach physically, but also mentally. He would make me feel as if I was going to be the strongest, the fastest, the toughest, and the smartest player there ever was. I loved that.

When we started working with Dave at a boxing gym, it wasn't long before he had us running through the streets of Covington, the town to the north of us. We called it our guerrilla workout. It was *tough.* And I loved every minute of it—me, the kid who hadn't wanted to run.

Coach Owen Hauck, our head coach, was a living legend. He came to Boone County High in 1979 and became the coach with the most wins in Kentucky high school history. From 1981 until 1997 he won twelve district titles, ten regional titles—and one state-at-large. If a team beat us in the playoffs, they'd win the state championship. The road to the state championship always had to pass through Boone County. Coach Hauck was great at getting players to be at their best when it counted.

During my sophomore year, Coach Hauck also brought in John Alford as the running back coach. John was only six years older than I was. He had been an outstanding running back at Boone County High, finished his career at Western Kentucky, and then decided to come back to his old high school to coach.

I liked John, and he treated me like his little brother. Any number of times after practice he'd say, "Let's go get something to eat, Shaun. We've got to get you some food 'cause you're too skinny." At the time I weighed 150 pounds.

John pushed me and worked with me, and by the following year my weight went up to 175, and in my senior year, I weighed in at 195. Of course, growth spurts helped, but I was putting on major pounds—working out, running, and also playing basketball.

One thing Coach Alford emphasized was the advantage of making the game fun. He had a great way of helping me do that. I'd be having a good game and he'd say, "You've got to get *better*, Shaun. Who cares if they can't stop you? You need seven touchdowns this week!"

Even now, after all these years, I appreciate his friendship and his advice.

In tenth grade, our star tailback at Boone County was Jason Colemire. He was *the man* at school. Jason was in my brother's class, and Durran and I often went over to his house and played basketball with him and his brother. Even in the winter when it snowed, we'd get out the shovels and clear the driveway so we could play. Sometimes we played till as late as two in the morning.

It was awesome for me to watch Jason play football. He made everything look effortless. I kept thinking, *I want to be a great athlete just like him.* But I knew I wouldn't be the team's running back because that's what Jason did, and he was outstanding in that position.

Now, as I look back, I realize God had already set me up to be respectful and to honor the guy who's in front of me. All through my football days, I've followed (and deeply respected) the outstanding players ahead of me. In college, I followed running backs who were designated All-SEC (Southeastern Conference). Later, I followed the great Ricky Watters, a five-time Pro-Bowler. I never resented that I came behind gifted players. I actually liked it, and I learned by watching them. I knew my time would come if I just patiently waited and watched.

During my sophomore year at Boone County, I played the role of loyal backup to Jason. I decided, though, that whenever I did get a chance to play, I'd go out there and rip the field up. I'd do my very best to shine.

I finally had a chance when we played against Dixie High School. I played hard and ended up with nine carries for 144 yards and four touchdowns. All through that game I kept thinking, *This is still easy*. Later that year we went to the state championships but lost the final game 3–0.

In my junior year, I was still Jason's backup. I expected it to be that way through the entire year, but that changed one Friday on game day. I was sitting in my computer class when some other students came in and told me, "Shaun, Jason just got hurt in gym class."

I had no idea how bad his injury was until one of the defensive ends, Brent Scudder, came to the classroom and motioned me out into the hallway.

As I reached the door, I asked, "Is it true about Jason?"

Brent nodded. "Yes, it's true. Shaun, you're going to have to carry us now."

He told me Jason had been playing dodgeball in the gym when he was slide-tackled by a substitute teacher. His knee was torn up pretty bad. "He'll be out for the rest of the season," Brent added.

I had mixed feelings because I wanted to play, but I didn't want to do it because of Jason's injury. But as I would learn, in sports that's how we often follow the previous man.

The team had 5 wins and 2 losses at that point in the year, so I felt some responsibility to keep us in a winning season. That evening we jumped on the bus and headed to Lexington to play against Lafayette High School. I was excited, but it still felt weird going into a game without Jason. It just didn't feel right.

My first carry in the game was a touchdown. So was my second. At halftime, I had 214 yards rushing and four touchdowns.

Coach Alford, who had set the Boone County High record for most yards in a single game when he was a player, came up to me and said, "Shaun, you're going to break my record!" But he was excited for me and cheered me on.

On my first carry in the third quarter, an opposing player tackled me and spun me around. I fell down and one of the guys fell on top of me. My teeth bit through my mouthpiece and went right through my lip. I was out for the rest of the game.

After the game they took me to the hospital, where they stitched me up. I still have a scar under my chin—the only scar I've ever earned from playing football.

That was my first official high school start as tailback: 221 yards, four touchdowns—and out of the game in the third quarter.

I had begun to play. For the rest of the season, I was our team's running back.

Chapter 4

NUMBER 37

n football, a player's number can become important. Great players may have their number retired when they quit the game. My number is 37, and when a lot of fans think of Shaun Alexander—they think of number 37.

But you'd be surprised at the way the number 37 has come to mean a lot more in my life than just being the number I wear on my back (I'll tell you that story in chapter seven). However, there's also a story in how I became number 37.

When I played peewee ball from second through sixth grades, I was given number 44. Then when I entered seventh grade, number 44 wasn't available, so I wore 48. When I played freshman ball I went back to 44.

When I entered Boone County High, they told me, "You can't be 44. The 40 numbers are reserved for our linebackers. You'll have to pick a different number." (That's when I learned that the team had a really good number 44, a linebacker named R.J. Riegler. If he hadn't been hurt, he probably would have earned a football scholarship.)

Fred Bernier, a former running back coach at Boone, helped me decide on the number that would stay with me from then on. He told me, "You ought to pick a number so that when anybody sees it, no matter where they are, that number will make them think of Shaun Alexander."

That sounded good to me.

I went through the locker room and looked over all the jerseys that were available. There were only two numbers I thought would always make people think of Shaun Alexander—either 9 or 37. As I was considering number 9, Durran told me about Tony Rice, the quarterback for Notre Dame who'd gone on to win the national championship. So I decided number 9 would always be his in the minds of football fans.

"What about 37?" I asked Durran. "Do you know anyone famous with that number?"

Durran couldn't think of any great 37s. Neither could I, nor could any of my friends. I pulled down that jersey and declared, "This will be my number—37."

That didn't sit well with everyone. One of my teammates didn't like the number. Another agreed: "You don't want to be 37—it's a terrible number. That's the number of a third-string fullback."

They were probably joking, but that only made me want it even more.

So I played my sophomore year as number 37 and kept the number all the way through high school and into college.

I didn't know it at the time, but numbering in the NFL system is set up so that running backs can have only the numbers 20 to 49. I was close to the middle of those numbers, and when I became a pro, I was able to keep my high school number.

And that's how I became number 37.

◆ ❖ ◆

During my junior year at Boone County High—the year I took over as tailback—I ended with a total of 2400 yards rushing and 42 touchdowns. I was good, but I didn't take my achievements for granted. I believed then, as I believe today, that God gave me a gift: an ability to play well. And I'm *very* grateful for that gift.

> "You'll go to a big college," Coach Murphy predicted, "and you'll play in the pros. You're going to have an outstanding career."

By late in that season I had begun to attract some fans. Of course, having fans was part of the fun and excitement, but I honestly didn't think of what I did as anything outstanding. I just seemed to be good at scoring touchdowns.

When we held our end-of-season banquet in February of 1994, I sat near Mike Murphy, a former pro player who had been one of my coaches. During the banquet he leaned over and said, "I understand you're getting a lot of letters from colleges."

"Yes, I have been," I said. I always knew I'd try to go on to college, but I had just started to realize I would actually be able to do it.

"You'll go to a big college," Coach Murphy predicted, "and you'll play in the pros. You're going to have an outstanding career, Shaun."

That was the first time a coach had ever said anything like that to me.

Playing football had never been a big dream of mine. That's what probably makes me different from many other players. Football was a sport I had started playing so I could have some fun with my brother and a friend, and it just turned out I was good at the game.

But Coach Murphy's words elated me. *My coach believed in me.* That started to open my eyes to a bigger picture.

The really amazing game of my junior year was our defeat of Campbell County High School. My first carry was a touchdown; the second was also a touchdown. I ended the game with 350 yards rushing and seven touchdowns.

That game was so unusual that the editors of *Sports Illustrated* put me in the front section of the feature called "Faces in the Crowd." I had already received a lot of letters from colleges, but that article put me on the national scene.

Two other things quickly followed. First, *Sports Illustrated* tagged me as the "Old Spice Athlete of the Month." The accompanying article featured a big picture of me with the caption "Mr. Touchdown." I thought that was awesome, because scoring touchdowns is what drives me on the field.

After that, ESPN followed me around for a week and featured me on *SSA* (Scholastic Sports America), their show about upcoming high school athletes. One thing I said on that show was, "I want to be the Michael Jordan of football. He puts up a lot of points. I want to be known for putting up a lot of points."

That really sums things up, because that's how I've always looked at football. It's a game I like, and I do love to score points.

After that good junior year, my senior year was even better. I ran for 3500 yards rushing, with 54 touchdowns. One of my favorite games from that year was the payback game against Lafayette High. They were a better team than we were—a lot better. They were having a great season and were boasting they would bust me up again—as they had in our previous match-up.

At the end of the first quarter, we were tied 7–7. Then in the second, third, and four quarters, I scored seven touchdowns. The game ended 81–7. That was one of the most fun games of my time playing football in high school.

I finished my high school football career with a total of 110 touchdowns (I had two games, including that Lafayette game, with seven touchdowns) and 6692 yards rushing.

My involvement with the Boone County High School football team didn't quite end when I stepped off the playing field for the last time. In April of 1995—the year I graduated—the school held a big pep rally during which they retired my jersey. It's unusual for a player to receive this honor while still a student, so I felt all the more excited about the award. I can't think of a more fantastic way to cap off a high school career. I was blessed.

Chapter 5

BIG DECISIONS

As I neared the end of my senior year, I had offers from colleges all around the country. I don't know how many letters I received—they seemed to come every day. I received them from Michigan, Alabama, USC, Notre Dame, and dozens of places I hadn't even known existed.

With so many colleges interested in me, I didn't know how to decide which one to attend, so I developed a technique that I know sounds crazy—but it worked for me. Here's what I did: I had stacks of letters in my room, and no matter which college it was that sent a letter, I tossed it over my left shoulder toward the wastebasket right behind my desk. If it landed inside the wastebasket, it stayed there. If it hit the floor, I picked it up and read it. Yes, that was crazy, but I just didn't know how else to do it. Every offer seemed good—but I had to choose only one, and this strange method worked.

By the time graduation was getting close, I had narrowed my choice to three: Notre Dame, Michigan, and Alabama. Notre Dame was on the list because of Durran. He was a freshman there when I was a senior in high school. Even though he wasn't a football player, he still loved the game, and Notre Dame had been the only school he had wanted to attend. Michigan was on the list because, like a typical little brother, I was interested in the college that was the rival of my brother's college. Besides, they had my favorite college player on their team—Desmond Howard.

As for Alabama—well, their scouts came to my high school and hung around with all the rest of the visiting scouts. They said they had a scholarship waiting for me, but then, other scouts—a lot of other scouts—said the same thing.

These scouts had all been coming regularly to watch me play. Their presence had become so common I'd stopped paying much attention to them. On occasion, I'd visited their schools and watched their teams play, and so I'd seen some of the best games of the season during my senior year of high school.

For example, I went to the Michigan/Colorado game and watched Kordell Stewart's Hail Mary pass to Michael Westbrook, who caught the ball in the back of the end zone to upset Michigan in the Big House.

There were all kinds of things said and done to try and influence my choice of a college. When a group of us seniors visited Notre Dame, their renowned head coach Lou Holtz said, "If all of you recruits will sign with us, we'll win the national championship four years in a row."

Hearing that, I got pumped as did the others.

One of the other guys joked, "Hey, he must know *I'm* here."

We all laughed. But really, we were all thinking the same thing. There *was* a lot of talent in that room. I particularly remember Fernando Bryant, who went to Alabama and later to the Jacksonville Jaguars. Reggie Grimes was there, though I didn't know it at the time. Reggie also would go to Alabama and was later signed as a rookie free agent by the Patriots. Charles Woodson went to Michigan before the Raiders drafted him. Randy Moss was in the room too—he went to Marshall, went on to play for the Vikings, and is now a Raider. Lou Holtz was right—if we'd all gone to Notre Dame, we probably would have won four years in a row.

But in 1999, who would have known so many of us would eventually become pro players? To most people we were just a bunch of 17- and 18-year-old kids full of dreams.

One day a coach I'd never heard of phoned and said, "I'm a representative of Tailback U. Do you know where that is?"

"I have no idea," I answered.

He laughed. "It's the nickname for the University of Southern California, and it's located in the heart of Los Angeles." Among other things, he told me they had more Heisman running backs than any other college. They had also won several championships.

"As a matter of fact," he continued, "we usually throw a barbeque for the best college running backs. I'd like to have you come and meet some people—you can come and meet the best running back ever."

"The best ever?" I asked. "Who was that?"

"Do you know Orenthal James Simpson?"

"You mean O.J. Simpson?" I exclaimed. "Who doesn't?"

He chuckled. "O.J. went to USC and he *was* the best. If you come to Tailback U, you're going to be part of that long tradition of great Trojan running backs."

I was pumped. The more he talked, the more excited I became about the possibility.

He said he'd send me a letter of invitation—and he did. But I hadn't counted on Mom. She was having none of that.

"No California school!" she said.

And that was that.

◆ ❖ ◆

Another possibility was Kentucky. People often ask me why I didn't go there, since it was only 35 minutes from my house. Here's why.

As soon as I walked into the office of the head coach, Bill Curry, I spotted a big championship ring on his desk.

"When did Kentucky win the championship?" I asked, surprised.

He laughed and told me, "This is a fake ring I made up so people can see what a championship ring looks like."

"Why is it so big?" I asked.

"Because when I get a lineman who can wear this ring," he said, "we're going to win a championship."

As a running back, I knew I would need a good offensive line. His remarks clued me in that Kentucky didn't have such a line. In contrast, I knew Michigan and Alabama already had big guys. The kind of guys who could give me the protection I'd need to score often. Right then I decided the University of Kentucky was out of the question.

During Christmas break of my senior year, several of my friends and I drove up to Michigan. Then we went to Notre Dame to see the campus again. I wanted to go back there one more time before I made up my mind.

While we were at Michigan, we had a great time. People showed us around the campus, and they impressed us with everything they had to offer. They were getting ready for a bowl game, so we watched the guys practice. Tyrone Wheatley and Tim Biakabutuka were the two best running backs in college at that time, and the Wolverines had just beat Ohio State. I stared like only a starstruck high school senior could.

Coach Gary Moeller talked to us and assured me I would love being a Wolverine. I didn't say yes, although I had just about decided to go there. I'm not sure what held me back.

When we drove down to Notre Dame, we went to Durran's dorm and met his roommates. Then we walked over to their football offices and waited for their bowl practices to start. While we were waiting, the running back coach walked past me and didn't say anything. A few seconds later, he walked past me again. None of the other coaches were there because they were out recruiting. This coach walked by me a third time and then a fourth.

Finally, the next time he approached, I reached out my hand and said, "Hi, how are you doing, sir?" As he shook my hand, I said, "I'm Shaun Alexander, a running back from Florence, Kentucky. I go to Boone County High School."

"Oh, hey—how you doin'?" he said. "Let me finish writing these messages on the coaches' board and I'll meet with you."

My friends and I followed him to a meeting room. As soon as he finished with the board, he sat down and talked with us for a few minutes.

"I guess you want to know what it's like to be a Notre Dame running back," he said. "Well, you've got to be able to break long runs, make big plays, catch, and throw. If you can do that, then I guess I could take you."

I guess I could take you.

My friends all looked at the man as if to ask, *Are you kidding?*

His words were deflating, but in a way, that was good for me. Until that moment, every school had treated me like a star. And now I didn't seem important to this man. I was surprised, but glad I found out before I made my decision. I needed to be on a team where I was wanted, not where they guessed they could take me.

Afterward, we walked back to Durran's dorm. My brother's college friends, who had been coming down to my high school games, were waiting there.

"Are you coming here?" they pressured me. "Are you coming?"

"No," I said. "I'm not going to come here."

"Why not?" they asked.

"I don't know," I replied. "The coach acted like he already has his running back."

They couldn't believe it.

"We need to *fire* that coach!" one of Durran's friends exclaimed.

I laughed. "You know that's just part of the game. Another thing—if God wanted me here, I'd feel excited about coming—and I don't."

The truth is, I had lost my excitement in that coach's office. In fact, it was the most crushing experience I'd ever had as a recruit. However, perhaps I needed it to happen so I could move out of the shadow of my big brother.

In February, we drove north to Ann Arbor so I could visit Michigan again. This would be my official visit. I was ready to sign, and I told my mom and my dad that if I enjoyed my visit as much as I was expecting to, I would sign with Michigan.

It took us almost five hours to travel what was normally a three-and-a-half-hour stretch. When we arrived, Ann Arbor had nearly three feet of snow on the ground—not three inches like often fell in our area, but three *feet*. I don't like snow, and the bad weather dampened my excitement a little. But something else happened on the visit that made it clear what my decision would be.

I went to a party attended by a large number of Michigan students. While there, I decided I'd ask some of them why they had chosen the school. I spotted one attractive girl and walked over to her. After we chatted a few minutes, we started to dance together.

"Why did you decide to attend Michigan?" I asked.

"Well," she replied, "it really wasn't my first choice. I wanted to go to another school, but I didn't get accepted." She shrugged. "Michigan accepted me, so I ended up coming here."

"Okay, that's cool," I said.

Later that night I asked another girl the same question: "Why did you decide to attend Michigan?"

"My whole family has gone here," she said. "I didn't even have to make a choice about it. I'm just following in my family's footsteps."

I talked to several more students while I was there. None of them seemed enthusiastic about their choice of college. The snow and their lack of excitement about Michigan badly dampened my enthusiasm.

A week later, both my parents went with me on the six-and-a-half hour drive to the University of Alabama in Tuscaloosa, which is close to Birmingham. The weather was beautiful, and people were bursting with warmth and a sense of confidence in their school.

I liked that.

Plus—in contrast to Michigan—all the students I spoke to at Alabama were proud of their football team, and it showed in the way they talked.

I also met a number of neat guys on that trip to Tuscaloosa. Guys who liked to have a good time—like any college students—but many of them were also Christians. That made the trip special. I met guys who loved football but also stood strong for what they believed. Every hour I was there, my enthusiasm increased.

Just like at Michigan, I went to a party while I was there. I decided to ask the same question I had asked those two girls in Ann Arbor. I walked up to a girl and asked, "Why did you choose Alabama?"

"This is the one college—the only college—I've wanted to attend," she told me. "It's just a fabulous school. We study hard, but we have so much fun—and everybody here loves the school."

I asked another girl—one of the most beautiful young women I'd ever seen—the same question.

"I love Alabama football!" was her sincere reply.

I smiled. "Enough said."

One more thing happened that made my decision clear. One of the Alabama players invited me to his church.

I had visited Vanderbilt, Kentucky, Michigan, and Notre Dame. I'd talked to coaches and players from several other schools. But only at Alabama did I meet anyone who talked to me about going to church.

As he spoke, I was thinking, *If I come here, I'll have friends who want to help me with my Christian walk.* That, plus the students' obvious love for their school, gave me two powerful reasons for signing with the Crimson Tide. It seemed obvious it was God's choice. I had prayed for God to show me the right school and to help me meet the right people, and He had.

> I had prayed for God to show me the right school and to help me meet the right people, and He had. By the time I was ready to go home, I wanted to ask, "Where are the papers?"

By the time I was ready to go home, I wanted to ask, "Where are the papers?" I didn't sign then, but I knew now that crimson was in my future. For me, the message was as clear as the Alabama slogan. God was saying, *Roll, Tide!*

◆ ❖ ◆

In March of 1995, as my senior year was nearing an end, I had my first press conference. This was the announcement where I would say that I had accepted a football scholarship. I think it was more of a big thing to my family and classmates than it was to me. Durran had even come home from Notre Dame to be with me.

I was more excited just to be going to college than about anything else.

The only people who knew my decision were my family and a few close friends. Most of the people at the press conference assumed I had chosen Notre Dame, although a few were sure it would be Michigan.

So when I announced, "I'm going to sign with Alabama," and my whole family took off their jackets and coats to reveal the Crimson Tide shirts they were wearing, the reaction was disbelief.

"What?" someone yelled.

I repeated my decision. And I got a huge laugh out of the whole thing because I had worn a crimson, white, blue, and green polo shirt so no one could figure out ahead of time from the colors I was wearing which school I had chosen. But after I made my announcement, I put on an Alabama cap, and I wore it almost every day after that.

◆ ❖ ◆

Not long after I agreed to go to Alabama on a scholarship, a representative from Florida State phoned. "We know you've verbally told Alabama you'll go there," he said. "But it's not yet signing day, and we have a situation here we think might interest you. We have two of the best college players in the country—the best quarterback and the best wide receiver. Like you, they'd verbally committed to attend different schools.

"Then both of them came to visit Florida State," the representative continued. "Once here, they realized that *we're* the school for them."

There was nothing illegal about what those two guys had done. Regardless of their stated intent, until players actually sign, they can change their minds.

"That's amazing," I said. "Who are the players?"

The man told me that the quarterback's name was Dan Kendra. I think he had planned to go to Penn State before he changed his mind. The receiver was Randy Moss, who had originally planned to enroll at Notre Dame.

"We want you, Shaun," the recruiter went on. "With you we'll have an unbeatable combination of the best receiver, the best quarterback, and you as the top running back."

"That's a nice honor," I told him, "and it feels good to have you call me the best—"

"You are, Shaun. That's why we want you and—"

"Although I really appreciate the offer," I said, interrupting his pitch, "I've given Alabama my word."

He started in again, reminding me I wasn't legally obligated. "You didn't write down anything," he said. "You didn't sign your name."

"I don't have to write it down to know what I said," I told him. "I said I would go to Alabama and that's what I meant. And that's what I'll do."

Once more he tried to talk me out of my decision, and he made a lot of promises of what Florida State would do for me.

I finally was tired of explaining, so I said, "Sir, thank you—but I'm not interested."

That time he accepted my answer.

My mother's teaching and the lessons I'd received as a kid in church were so strong, I didn't even feel tempted. To give my word is as strong as signing a contract. I couldn't go back on that.

A couple of weeks later, I signed with Alabama and began to get ready for the most important times of my life. And I was sure glad that the Alabama letter I had tossed over my shoulder hadn't landed in the wastebasket!

◆ ❖ ◆

High school graduation finally came. And with graduation came the parties and the goodbyes. I smiled often, but I felt weird. Emotionally, I knew I had to leave soon…and I would miss everybody.

I would miss my dad as well. Even though just about everything in our relationship was bittersweet, he'd started coming to my games during my sophomore year. When we would get off the field, he'd ask, "Hey, Shaun, what do you want to do after the game?"

Usually I'd say, "I'm hungry."

So we'd often go to a little restaurant in Florence called the Ground Round, near the movie theaters on Mall Road. I liked these times with my dad. It felt like he really wanted to spend time with me.

My friend Brian Maney and his dad usually came along too, and I liked that. Over the next year or so, our dads became good friends.

We went to that little restaurant after every home game. Through my junior year, it was just something we did. By my senior year, however, going to the Ground Round had become an event. It seemed like the more games we won, the more the news seemed to spread about our going to the Ground Round. After each game, the crowds would get bigger.

Brian and I and our dads would walk in after we had beaten another school.

"Great game, boys!" someone would yell.

"Boone County wins another!" somebody else would call out as people clapped and cheered. "Shaun Alexander blows the Rebels to victory again!"

I loved the attention. But I especially liked it that my dad was there being a part of it. Even now, I still miss those father-and-son moments—with Dad standing at my side as we walked in and listened to the cheering. His presence made everything special.

I knew I would miss my friends a lot too. I had known most of those kids since I had started school, and those of us who'd played football together had formed awesome friendships.

I had chosen Alabama, but none of my close friends from high school would be going with me. That was disappointing, but they had to make their decisions just as I did. Brian Maney enrolled in a community college, Ray Arnold went to Western Kentucky, Josh Hays started his career in the restaurant business, and Scott Woodall went to the University of Kentucky.

Separation time meant we would be taking separate paths. That was rough, but we vowed we'd always stick together, although far apart. And we have kept that commitment. To this day, we still call each other regularly. Even now, I can call up one of those guys and within two minutes, I feel as if I'd never left Florence, Kentucky.

Chapter 6

'BAMA CALLS

I want to be clear I didn't go to Alabama just to play football. No matter how good a player is—even if he makes it into the pros—his career doesn't last long. As I later learned, the average pro football career lasts about four years. I didn't know how long mine would last if a professional team drafted me, but I wasn't going to depend on football. I wanted an education.

But I was there to play too. During my freshman year, however, I was "redshirted." When students are redshirted, it means they're on the team and they practice and live like players, but they don't play in any games. The next year they're called redshirt freshmen—and they can still play for four years. The rule at every university is that a student gets five years to play four years of football. If he does it right, he can graduate and still have the summer and a full semester to play. Some students use that extra time to get started on their master's degrees. Others use the time to add another major or minor as an undergraduate if they have already received their first degree.

❖ ❖ ❖

When I first arrived at Alabama in the fall of 1995, I was feeling pretty cool. I was grown up and on my own. Still, my upbringing held me in good stead, and in getting settled in Tuscaloosa, I remembered two things my mother had said to me: "Find a good church. Find good friends."

My hunt for a good church started the first day I arrived on campus. The one thing I wanted was a pastor who would teach me what the Bible says and show me how to follow its teachings better.

One day, I heard a couple of classmates talking about what they had learned at their church. My ears perked up, and I asked one of them where he went to church.

"Calvary Baptist," he replied. "It's the best church I've ever attended."

"Where is it?" I asked.

He stared at me as if I were a little stupid. "It's right next to the stadium."

"Cool. I'll be there Sunday," I said.

I had come from a church with maybe 150 people present on a good Sunday. In contrast, Calvary Baptist held two services, and there must have been a thousand people there on any given Sunday. My first impression was that the congregation was predominantly white. I had come from an all-black church, filled with excitement and praise, and where people sang with all their hearts. I was used to a heavily emotional service where people expressed themselves unreservedly from their hearts.

So needless to say, I was shocked that first Sunday at Calvary Baptist. I'll just say the music was nothing like what I'd heard every Sunday since childhood.

What am I doing here? I asked myself about halfway through the service. When I had almost made up my mind not to come back, the pastor, Dr. Bruce Chesser, stood up and started to preach. As I listened, I could hardly believe how his words captivated me. He was spellbinding. I felt as if God was speaking directly to me and telling me how to live. This was the kind of preaching I had been yearning for.

This is where I belong. I knew that then. I still didn't like the music, but the preaching was exactly what I needed. But instead of hurrying to church as I had done all through my childhood to enjoy the worship and praise, I'd enter the building just in time to hear Dr. Chesser speak. For the first year at Calvary Baptist, that became my pattern.

◆ ❖ ◆

My second year at Alabama, I played a couple of good games for the Crimson Tide and started to be recognized at church. The few times I arrived at the church early, people would come over and talk to me, especially the kids. They would smile and say, "Hey, I know who you are," and ask for my autograph. Even during the service, it wasn't unusual for a kid to slip over to me and hand me something to sign. That didn't feel right to me, but I understood.

In hopes of avoiding any distraction, I decided I would sit in a different place every Sunday. Should I sit up in the main balcony? On the side balcony? Closer to the front? That became my big Sunday morning decision.

One day I saw a boy, maybe nine years old, sitting alone in a pew. I sat down next to him. Surprisingly, he didn't say one word to me during the service. I appreciated that. I was able to listen to Dr. Chesser without any distraction.

The next week when I came into the church, I looked for the same boy. I decided he'd be perfect to sit next to because he didn't talk to me or ask for an autograph. He listened intently to the pastor, and I liked that.

I found him and sat next to him. He still didn't say anything to me. When I got up to leave that second Sunday, I turned to him and said, "I like sitting next to you. Save me a spot next week, okay?"

"Sure!" he said with a grin.

The next week, I walked in, and sure enough, he had saved me a place. I sat down, smiled, and both of us focused on the service. I didn't talk to him, and he didn't talk to me. I was able to listen to everything and not be distracted.

After about a month, I turned to him at the end of the service and asked him his name.

"I'm Kyle," he said.

"And I'm Shaun."

"Yeah, I know who you are," Kyle said. "You're a good football player."

"Thank you." I smiled and waited to see if he was going to ask for an autograph or want to talk. He didn't say anything. Again, I liked that.

For the next two Sundays I'd come in and say, "How you doing, Kyle?" And he'd smile as I sat down in the place he'd saved for me. That was it.

One Sunday, as soon as the pastor gave the benediction, Kyle said, "My mom and dad take college kids out to eat for this college program."

"College program? What do you mean?" I asked.

"You're not from around here, are you?" he said.

"No, I'm not."

"See, it's like this," he explained. "Our church has an 'adopt-a-college-student' ministry, where they take in college students who don't have families nearby. They can go out to eat with people or get a home-cooked meal and stuff like that."

"That's a good idea," I said and started to walk away. I didn't know if he was inviting me or just giving me information.

"So do you want to go eat lunch with us?" I saw the excitement in his eyes, but I hesitated.

He didn't say anything more. He just waited for my answer.

"Well, I *am* hungry," I admitted.

"Come on then," he said. "I'll introduce you to my mom and dad." With that, he grabbed my hand and pulled me toward the back of the church. There he introduced me to his parents, Lee and Lucy Sellers, his older sister, Leah, and Kristen, who was his younger sister. As I learned, there was a regular group the Sellers took out every Sunday for lunch, or else they would arrange something at their house for the college kids. I thought, *This is such a great idea*. I didn't know it then, but the Sellers would be a major influence in my life and would become my family away from home.

I liked going out to eat with the Sellers on Sunday, and through them I was introduced to lots of other students. During those times of being together, I would watch the other students and the Sellers children. They were different in the way they talked. The best way I can explain it is to say that they were more into a right relationship with God than they were into just attending church. Even though I wasn't aware of it for a long time, by their attitudes and commitment they challenged me to grow spiritually.

That first lunch would be followed by many such lunches. That lasted for just about every Sunday I was in Tuscaloosa.

As my spiritual life grew and my studies continued, I was also playing well and beginning to set new school records. Even though more people wanted to hang around me as I became more famous in town, I stuck with Kyle and the Sellers.

There must have been about 20 of us regulars from the university who hung with the Sellers family. We all became friends and did things together at other times during the week, not just on Sunday. For instance, one weekend several of these new friends took me along with them and taught me how to water-ski.

But the most important lesson I learned during this time was how a good marriage works. It was the first time I ever saw a couple disagree and didn't feel like they were headed toward a divorce court. Not only had my parents divorced when I was a kid, but I had observed almost no role models for a good marriage. Even in the homes of some of my friends I'd heard couples scream at each other, make threats, and walk away blazing with anger. The Sellers weren't like

> **Because of their example…they unknowingly caused me to reach a decision about my future. When I finished college and had a job, I decided, I wanted to make reaching out to kids a priority in my life.**

that, and they set a great example for me—probably without realizing it.

Also, although my mom was a loving person and a great disciplinarian, this was the first time I'd ever seen a *father* as the family disciplinarian. At 18 years old, what I saw in the Sellers made a powerful impact on me.

When I get married, this is the kind of relationship I want, I vowed.

I also felt close enough to the Sellers to ask them questions. I asked Lee about dating and about girls. I didn't know exactly how he thought about me, but the way he and Lucy treated me made me feel as if I were the oldest son in their house. But then, they made all of us college kids feel like we were part of their family.

Because of their example of opening their home and their hearts to far-from-home students, they unknowingly caused me to reach a decision about my future. When I finished college and had a job, I decided, I wanted to make reaching out to kids a priority in my life. There's no price tag on what we do for others—that's what that generous family taught me. I constantly thank God for using them to show me this truth.

After college, when I left Alabama, I didn't leave the Sellers. Their influence is still deep in my heart, and they still are opening their arms and hearts to college kids, providing food and opportunities to be around a family—a warm, loving family. I regularly send them team clothing and other gifts. That's my way to tell them I still love them.

When I had my draft party in Cincinnati—more about that later—they drove all the way up from Tuscaloosa. There are always certain people we like to have around, even if things are so busy we don't have time for deep conversations. The Sellers are like that.

Down the road, when I had some money, I visited them—and one of the reasons was because I wanted to take *them* out to eat as a kind of repayment for all the meals they had provided for me. At the end of the meal, I asked for the check.

Lee frowned at me. "What are you doing, Shaun?" he asked.

"I'm treating *you*," I replied.

"No, you're not," he answered. He didn't care how much money I had, he still wanted to provide for *me*.

And to this day, he has never willingly let me pay for a family meal. (A few times I've been able to sneak the bill from the waiter and act as if nothing's going on, but Lee always protests.)

I wish I could do more for them. But then, there's never any way to repay kindness and love—except to pass it on.

That's what I try to do.

At the beginning of this chapter, I mentioned two things my mother told me to do at Alabama. The first was to find a good church. The second was to find good friends.

Shortly after I arrived, I met Kendrick Burton and Brad Ford, who were seniors, as well as Toderick Malone and Shannon Brown. These great guys became some of my first friends on campus. Kendrick would later become an influential person in my life, especially after I started my career.

Being redshirted back then, I wasn't playing, just practicing—and that was all right with me. I wanted to become a better player, grow up a little, and enjoy my first months in college. Some of my classmates helped me do that—Fernando Bryant, Michael Moore, Shamari Buchanan, Chris Samuels, and my roommate, Reggie Grimes. I also hung with Brian Cunningham, Brandon Turner, and Michael Gurley. We did a lot of crazy things together.

Reggie, my roommate, and I were the same age. While I was a senior at Boone County High, he was at Hunters Lane High School in Nashville. Both of us took trips to the same colleges to watch football games, but we'd never met before we started to room together. Reggie took me in as if I were his little brother. He wasn't older—but he was bigger. He weighed 250 pounds to my 200. I'm six feet tall, but he towers over me by at least four inches. He'd introduce me to his friends as his "home dog."

One day we got to talking about the college games we had seen when we were in high school.

"I went to the Notre Dame/Michigan game," Reggie said. "Lou Holtz was there, and he talked about all the great talent."

"You were in that room *too?*" I was floored. "*I* was there." Then I told him about the time I'd attended the Michigan/Colorado game with Kordell Stewart's winning Hail Mary pass.

"I was at that game too," he said, grinning.

We just laughed over the whole thing. We'd both been at the same games any number of times, but we'd never met. Yet both of us ended up playing for Alabama and rooming together. We felt as if we should have known each other earlier.

Reggie was a great roommate, and like I said, we became like brothers. We'd go to his family's house in Nashville or he would come up to Florence with me. I've heard some bad stories about how roommates constantly fight or despise each other. But during our four years together, we had only one major problem—and I caused it.

Reggie had great clothes, and I liked his taste. Sometimes he'd leave in the morning, and I'd put on his clothes and wear them to class. He didn't catch me—when I'd come in from class, he'd be napping. My borrowing his clothes went along just fine—for a while.

Then one day it rained, and I had to run across the campus. I forgot I was wearing Reggie's suede jacket. When I arrived back at our dorm, I started brushing the soaked jacket. Then I looked up. There stood my six-foot-four-inch roommate. He was mad, but all he did was give me a warning: "Don't do it again, Shaun."

That was enough. I never borrowed his jacket again. (Notice I said "jacket." I must admit I *did* continue to borrow his other clothes.)

Yes, Reggie was a great friend. One of the things I'm grateful for is that he taught me how to drive a stick shift. He owned a red Maxima, and he patiently taught me how to shift the gears. When both of us thought I understood how to do it, he let me use his car to run errands.

One afternoon I went to the store to pick up a few groceries and then did some driving around. I thought I smelled something burning and pulled over. Rod Rutledge, one of our tight ends, came up in his car and asked, "Is that coming from your car? I could smell it half a block away."

"Yeah, but I don't know what it is," I said.

He got out and looked inside. "It's the brake, man," he said. He pointed to the lever. "Put the brake down." I had left the emergency brake up while I was driving, and I couldn't figure out why I couldn't punch the gears like before.

I thanked Rod and drove back to the dorm. Of course I was pretty embarrassed, but I thought this would be Rod's and my little secret.

I was wrong.

Rod thought it was funny and told someone who told someone else, and it got back to Reggie before I even got back to our room. I apologized, but he had a hard time letting me drive his car after that. One day, he finally asked me to take his car and run an errand. Then I knew he had really forgiven me. I was truly blessed to have such a compatible roommate.

One time during my redshirt freshman year, Reggie was gone somewhere in his Maxima, and I didn't have transportation. I was hungry and wanted something to eat. I walked down the hallway looking for some of the other players but couldn't find them. (All of us on the football team lived in Bryant Hall—named in honor of the legendary coach, Bear Bryant.)

As I was coming back toward my room, I saw Michael Gurley and Michael Crocker in their room, which was diagonally across the hall from me.

I asked them, "You guys hungry?"

Gurley, who was one of our student trainers, looked up. "Yeah," he said, "…and I'll drive."

I smiled because I hadn't even had to ask.

We jumped into his Toyota and drove over to Burger King, where we ate and then talked for a while.

That evening began a pattern. Almost every night around midnight, Mike Gurley and I went out to eat. Burger King stayed open late, so we'd meet in the hallway and take off. We hadn't been close before, but going out to eat regularly like that made us good friends. Our relationship grew, and Mike and I became tight.

Of all the nonplayers, Mike was definitely my closest guy friend, and we did a lot of things together. One Thanksgiving he took me to meet his family, who lived about a 40 minutes' drive from campus. After that, we went about once a week for a visit to his family.

◆ ❖ ◆

When I think about my good friends, there's no way I can ever forget Phyllis Billingsley and Heather Neighbor, who were two of the best.

The first class of my freshman year was political science. As I walked into the classroom, I wondered who I'd sit next to. I looked around and saw a girl I recalled meeting briefly during my recruiting trips. She was laughing and smiling and cracking jokes and seemed to be having fun with her friends.

The seat next to her was empty so I sat down and said, "Hi, I'm Shaun."

"Hi, I'm Bonnie Fay," she said. Everyone around her laughed at that, and so did I, though I had no idea what was so funny.

She cracked some more jokes and then the class began.

When the class was over, I walked with her out of the classroom, and another girl said to her, "Bye, Phyllis."

"Bye-bye," she replied.

"I thought your name was Bonnie Fay," I said.

She laughed and shook her head. "No, I'm Phyllis Billingsley."

As I was to learn, Phyllis was a wonderful person—a great joker—and one of the funniest people I've ever been around. She could make anyone laugh.

During my second semester, I met Heather Neighbor at a college gathering at Calvary Church. She was the first girl I'd ever met who I felt was like me in many ways. We became good friends, and we often stayed up late talking, going to parties, and critiquing each other's dates.

I felt closer to Heather than I ever had to any other girl. It was not at all a romantic friendship. To the contrary, I used to think of her as my guardian angel. She pushed other girls away to keep me from the wrong types.

Phyllis and Heather became my close female friends, and I enjoyed being with them throughout my time at Alabama.

In Florence, Kentucky, my high school had been predominately Caucasian. Most of the girls I had dated were white. At Alabama I was meeting a greater diversity of women—including more African-American women. It was great to be around so many different kinds of women: smart, charming, fast, slow, innocent, wild. I saw light-skinned girls and dark-skinned girls. And as I met and dated more black women, I began to realize that the kind of woman I wanted to marry would be confident, smart, and independent—and she would know that about herself.

In my dating, I was still following the same limits I had set in high school. I want to repeat what my mother had taught me: to never exploit women—that sex was meant only for marriage—and to treat all women with respect. I knew the boundary lines, and I knew it wasn't right to cross them.

In the Bible, there's a verse that talks about treating "younger women as sisters, with absolute purity."* That's a Scripture I decided to stand on. I knew if I didn't keep my focus, I could fall. And it could occur anytime.

One time it almost did.

It happened that first year of college when I had gone home for a visit.

To protect her privacy, I'll call her Sherron. One night we were alone in my room while my mom was gone. We were kissing, and I thought seriously about having sex with her. But something in me kept whispering, *This isn't right.*

Just then the phone rang. It was my mother, and she asked, "Is everything good, Shaun?"

"Uh...yeah, Mom," I said. "It's good."

"What's going on?" she asked.

"Oh, nothing," I answered. "Sherron is here and we're going to go out and eat and probably go to a movie. Something like that."

"Okay, that's fine," Mom said. "I'm going to stay in Covington with your grandma, so I'll call you tomorrow."

As I hung up, thoughts raced through my mind. *What am I doing here? Something isn't right about this. This is so easy and nobody else will know. But I'll know, and God will know.* It was more than wrestling with my thoughts. I was in a full-out fight. I had to decide who my body would serve.

Just then, Sherron leaned close to me and whispered, "I've brought condoms."

My thoughts were racing. Mainly I was thinking, *Am I one of those rotten guys who says he loves Jesus but folds when it's easy or when he knows he won't get caught?*

"No, we can't do this," I finally said.

"Why not?"

"We're not supposed to."

"What does *that* mean?" Sherron asked.

I jumped up and pulled her to her feet. "It means we're going out."

I hurried her out to the car, and we drove to the mall. That was the closest I ever got to having sex before marriage.

Mom's phone call had kept me from making a big mistake. Many times I've been grateful to my mother for calling exactly when she did. But then,

---

* 1 Timothy 5:2.

that's one of the wonderful things about my mother—somehow she knew the right time to call. Or God knew the right time to urge her to call.

◆ ❖ ◆

That was not the first time I had to decide who I was going to serve. Here I'll jump ahead a little to my junior year. I was really trying to figure out what was going on in my life and where I wanted to go with it. I realized I wasn't as focused as I thought I should be. Sure, I did well in my classes, studied hard, and pulled high grades. I had decent stats and my football work was fine, but I still wasn't satisfied with my spiritual life.

> I realized I was so busy looking to the left and right that I was missing what was in front of me. I had been distracted by other things. I needed to turn my focus on to God.

Anyone who knew me would have called me a Christian, maybe even a committed one. I looked like one. I went to church, prayed, and read my Bible—all the things I had been taught to do. But something was missing.

About that time, I read and memorized a verse from the book of Joshua: "Be strong and very courageous. Be careful to obey all the law my servant Moses gave you; do not turn from it to the right or to the left, that you may be successful wherever you go."

Those words hit me hard. I had been careful to obey the laws of God. I could stand up for what was right, and I hadn't compromised. As I thought through those words, however, I also realized two new things. First, if I did everything God told me to do, I would be successful. (I don't equate being successful with having a lot of money or being famous, but with living a good life.)

The second thing that struck me was that one phrase: "Do not turn from it to the right or to the left." Theologians may tell me I didn't understand the message—I can only say that God spoke to me and convinced me of something as I repeated those words day after day. Not only was I not to *go off* the path, the command was to not even *turn*. As I kept pondering that verse and the entire chapter from Joshua, I realized I was so busy looking to the left and right that I was missing what was in front of me. I had been distracted by other things. I needed to turn my focus onto God.

The words of Joshua chapter one were hard for me to put into action, but I knew I had to obey. For a couple of days I kept thinking, *I want to go for God's definition of success.*

And I began to change. Up until then, I'd felt like I had done the things I was supposed to do with three-quarters of a heart or half a heart. I didn't like being that way, because my philosophy was, "If I'm going to do it, I go all out."

Now, though, the spirit of excellence was at work. God became my focus—the center of my life.

Chapter 7

PSALM 37:4

My first playing season—in 1996—was the last year for head coach Gene Stallings. I started the season as the third-team running back behind Curtis Alexander (no relation) and Dennis Riddle. My first carry came against Bowling Green in the season opener. I rushed six times for 19 yards, and Alabama won 21–7.

I scored my first touchdown against the Kentucky Wildcats, when I ran ten yards for the game's first score. We trounced them 35–7.

Nothing really remarkable happened during my first eight games, though I did move up to second team after Curtis fractured his left wrist in a game against Arkansas. Overall, I had 28 carries for 144 yards. Our team had a 7 and 1 record, our only loss being to Tennessee.

At that point, I was just another player who showed promise. However, during this time, something else happened that would radically change my life and get me ready for the refocusing I mentioned in the previous chapter. And it was more about the number 37.

At just the age of 19 I was meeting many new people—great people who would profoundly influence my life. One of these men was Jeff Reitz, an assistant strength coach—and a great man of God. He and other strong believers on the team began challenging me to read my Bible more regularly.

"You're a real good kid," Jeff told me. "You don't drink, you don't wild out, you don't fool around with the girls, and you're not into drugs. You're a good Christian kid, but you need to grow."

"Grow?" I asked. "What are you talking about?"

"Here's the math problem," he said. "Every day you're either spending time with Jesus or you're spending it with Satan. We have seven days in every week. If you're only going to read your Bible, pray, and worship God on Sunday, how many days a week are you with the Lord?"

"One," I said.

"Right," Jeff answered. "And how many days are you with Satan?"

I started laughing. "Okay—I got you, Jeff. Cool."

Then he continued, "You go to the weekly FCA (Fellowship of Christian Athletes) meetings on Wednesday nights. Now—how many days of each week do you spend with the Lord?"

"Two."

"How many days with Satan?"

"Five."

"Right. And there's no way you can give two of something and go against five of something and still win."

I agreed. "So what do you do?" I asked.

"Every day I get up and I read my Bible, Shaun," he said. "I encourage you to do the same. It doesn't have to be a whole lot, just a little something. And once a week I try to memorize a Scripture verse."

It sounded good to me. I had never done much in the way of memorizing Bible verses, but I was willing to try.

A few weeks after our conversation, Jeff asked, "Shaun, are you reading your Bible more?"

"Yeah…" I said. I really hadn't read much, but at least I had started.

The next week Jeff came up to me again, put his hand on my shoulder, and asked me the same question.

"No," I said, "I haven't read more yet."

He didn't say anything.

He didn't need to say anything. So I read a little bit most days; some days I didn't. I wasn't consistent. The other Christian guys were patient with me and tried hard to help me add this daily habit to my life.

At this time I was also getting more involved with FCA, and one of the guys there was also challenging me, just like Jeff was. He gave me the same message: "I'll tell you what, Shaun—you need to read something from the Bible *every* day."

"Yeah—I know, I know," I replied. "I want to do that but I'm not sure what to read."

He thought for a moment. "Okay, since 37 is your number, why don't you read everything in the Bible with the number 37 in it?"

I didn't get it. I asked, "Is the number 37 mentioned in the Bible?"

He laughed. "No, I mean in every book of the Bible that has a chapter 37, read that chapter as well as every verse 37 you find in the chapters."

I shrugged. "Yeah, I can do that."

"So read something with 37 in it *every day*," he said. "You can start with Genesis 1:37, Genesis 2:37. Go on to chapter 37 and keep on going. Read everything numbered 37."

"Okay, I'll do that," I promised.

It worked, though I didn't always understand what I was reading. Some of those verses didn't make sense when taken out of context. But I did it anyway because it was good discipline for me.

A couple of weeks later, one of the Christian guys asked me, "Okay, Shaun—are you reading from the Bible every day?"

"Actually, I am," I said.

"That's good," he said. "Have you ever memorized a verse from Scripture before?'

"Yeah, sure," I said. I quoted John 3:16: " 'God so loved the world that he gave his one and only Son, that whoever believes in him shall not perish but have eternal life.' That's all I know," I said.

"That's a good beginning," he said. "But do you know the importance of memorizing Scripture?"

"Tell me."

"The truth is, one day everything will die," he said. "The trees outside will die. My car engine will die, and even you and I will die one day. The only thing that lives forever is the Word of God. So when you memorize Scripture, you make the Word part of your heart that will live forever."

No one had ever said that to me before. I liked the sound of it.

"So if you memorize Scripture," he continued, "you're going to be able to make more of a place for God inside your heart. The more you know, the more you're going to be able to walk it out and live a consistent life. The words in your heart will keep you on the right path."

He continued for a few minutes and then said something that really struck home: "Find one verse that speaks to you, and make that your life verse." He suggested, "Your number is 37, Shaun, so try this: Memorize whatever you like in the Bible that has the number 37 in it." I was already reading "37s" in the Bible, so this seemed like a good idea.

And interestingly, I found some really cool things I liked, such as Luke 1:37: "Nothing is impossible with God." That's tight, and I really liked it—but I knew it wasn't what I wanted to be my life verse.

"Read until you find that special Scripture with 37 in it," my friend later advised me. "Every time you read that verse, it'll remind you of how good God is."

For days, those words echoed in my mind, along with the other things he'd said: "Your life verse will also remind you of your relationship with God. And when folks who know that's your verse read that Scripture, they'll think of you and your relationship with God. It'll all go back to God."

◆ ❖ ◆

The next weekend we were playing LSU. Before the game, we were 7 and 1, as I said. On Monday, I raced up to my room thinking about this life verse idea. *I just need to pick the verse that best fits my life,* I said to myself. I read Psalm 37 several times, thinking I'd find my verse there, but nothing clicked.

We practiced that day, and it went all right. During Tuesday's practice, though, something was wrong with me. I fumbled early, and later I ran the wrong direction—when the quarterback called the play to run to the left, I ran to the right. Ivy Williams was a tough coach and one of the best I've ever had. He'd coached other football greats, including Barry Sanders. That day he yelled, "Shaun, get out of the huddle! Get out of the drill. I can't believe I recruited a kid from Kentucky. I'll probably never recruit another kid from your state again."

I felt awful. I didn't know what was wrong with me. I stayed on the sideline, trying to have the best day possible for a guy who had just been chewed out like that by a great coach.

On Saturday, we had walk-throughs in the morning, and that afternoon we were going to get on the team plane and fly to Baton Rouge to play LSU.

And that was the day I found the verse I wanted—a verse I had read through many times. In fact, it had been in Psalm 37 all along. The very chapter I'd been looking at without success. But for some reason, *now* this Scripture was clicking with me—and since that day it has been my life verse.

We had boarded the plane, and I looked up to see John David Phillips, the sophomore backup quarterback on our team. "J.D.," I told him, "I found my life verse."

"What is it?" he asked.

As I was about to tell him, the older guys told us to sit down so we could take off. "I'll tell you when we land," I said to J.D.

For some reason that didn't happen when we arrived in Baton Rouge.

We went to our hotel, where my roommate was Montoya Madden, the fourth-string tailback. I was the third-string, and we were the young guns—he was a sophomore and I was a redshirt freshman.

In our first meeting there at the hotel, when the coach had his back to us, Montoya nudged me. "Man, he's talking like we ain't even gonna get in the game."

"Naw, we're going to get in the game," I whispered back. "I'll show you."

I raised my hand. "Hey, Coach—when they line up in this defense we're going to audible to this play?"

Coach put his hands on his hips and stared at me. "Don't worry about it, Shaun," he said.

I whispered to Montoya, "I guess you're right. We're not going to play."

After we wrapped up the meeting, we hurried up to our room. All the way Montoya kept saying, "I can't believe we're not going to play."

I was smart enough to realize he was setting me up for something, but I couldn't figure it out. He was like that.

But the answer wasn't far off.

Montoya had brought his PlayStation. We both liked video games, so we started to play Coach K, the college basketball game. The night passed so quickly that we had no idea what time it was until we heard a knock on the door. When I opened it, our assistant coach was there. "All right, boys—lights out," he said.

"We really don't need to go to sleep because we ain't gonna play in the game anyway," I told him. "We're going to stay up and play video games for a while."

What I wanted him to answer was, "No, don't do that. We're going to need you because you're going to play."

Instead, he glanced at me and then at Montoya and said, "Yeah, you're probably right. Okay, but don't wake up any of the players." And with that, he shut the door.

The two of us finished the game, and I won by a buzzer shot. I was ready to go to bed, but Montoya said, "Let's play it again."

We did, and this time he won by a buzzer shot.

So we played a third game, and I won again by a buzzer shot.

"This is crazy," Montoya exclaimed. "Let's play again." By that time he was ready to play all night—and so was I.

We played more games than I could keep count of. The one thing I recall is that I ended up whipping him pretty good. After I had won still another game, I looked at the clock. It was nearly 3:30. "Oh, man," I said, "we've been up all night."

"We'd better get some sleep," he replied. Both of us knew we had a wake-up call at 7:00.

"Don't worry about sleep," I told him. "We'll get up, go to breakfast, and sleep between meetings." Our game wasn't until 8 PM.

"Great idea!" he said.

We went to bed. When we woke up less than three hours later, we made our way down to breakfast and on to the first team meeting.

"Hey, we heard you guys were up all night," one of the older linemen said.

"The word is that you were playing PlayStation," another added.

"Yeah, we were," Montoya admitted. "Shaun beat me pretty bad."

"I'll bet I could beat you," the one lineman said.

Before we realized what was happening, we agreed to a challenge from the two of them. So we ended up playing through the first sleeping break. We didn't stop playing until it was time for lunch.

After lunch, we had another meeting before getting back to our rooms. This time I was determined I would sleep.

"Aw, what difference will it make?" one of the players asked. "You're not going to play in the game tonight. Even the coach said so."

Dennis Riddle, the starting running back, and Curtis Alexander, the backup running back, were already in our room playing games. Before we knew it, fullbacks Ed Scissum and Trevis Smith had joined us. Montoya and I decided we might as well stay up, so we missed our last opportunity to sleep before the game.

When it was time, we went down for the pregame meal. Afterward we boarded the bus for the stadium. I slumped into my seat and closed my eyes. The next thing I remember was jerking awake when several LSU fans pushed against our bus and screamed, "Tiger bait! Tiger bait!"

I followed the others out of the bus and into the locker room. I was so tired, I put on my practice cleats instead of my game cleats. I should have changed, but I was just dead. I knew I wasn't going to play in the game anyway, so I decided I might as well be comfortable. I didn't change my cleats and didn't put on all the parts of my shoulder pads. Why should I? I just wanted to relax.

I glanced over at Montoya. He was so tired that he was trying to put his left practice cleat on his right foot. "Here's what we're going to do," I said to him. "We'll go out of the tunnel and do what every freshman does—we'll pump up the crowd, and once the game gets going, we'll slide back to the bench and act like we're studying the chalkboard. Then we'll be able to sit down."

"Oh, man—that's a great idea," he replied.

At the end of the first quarter, the score was 0–0. We were playing a good defensive game, but our offense couldn't get going. When the second quarter started, we drove hard down the field. Dennis ran the ball, was hit, and grabbed his leg in pain.

"You all right?" Coach Williams yelled. "Are you all right?"

It was obvious he *wasn't* all right. He turned and hobbled to the bench.

"Alexander!" the coach shouted.

I jumped up. My heart was going a hundred beats a second.

"No—get out of the way, Shaun." It turned out he meant *Curtis* Alexander, not me. "Curtis, get over here!"

Curtis ran out on the field. Our offense approached the line of scrimmage. There were only five seconds left on the clock to call the play, so our quarterback called time-out, and the team rehuddled.

"Call the play the other way," Coach Williams directed. "Curtis has a cast on his left hand. Call the play the other way." Though they wanted to run the play to the left, Curtis's cast would have made it hard for him to carry the ball in his left hand.

The offense returned to the line of scrimmage, but when ESPN wanted to run commercials, they returned to the huddle again.

> "Alexander, we're going to make a hole for you. Even if you have to close your eyes, run—and run *hard!*"

The coach whipped around. "Alexander, go in there!"

"*Me?*" I was so surprised I couldn't think of anything else to say.

He nodded and pointed toward the huddle. Curtis came out. I went in and we ran the play to the left. As I ran, some guy fell, and the next thing I knew I'd jumped over him. Then I was hit—and slid into the end-zone cone. One carry, 17 yards, and one touchdown.

When halftime came, we were ahead of LSU 7–0—and I was still wearing my practice cleats. We really wanted this game because the winner would probably go on to play in the SEC championship game, and maybe even move on to play for the national championship.

During the break, Coach Williams was standing at the chalkboard and writing a play while we sat in our semicircle. Then he paused, turned around, and said, "Shaun, great run."

I grinned. I felt really good at that compliment because only days earlier, he had told me I was the last kid from Kentucky he'd ever recruit.

When we went back out for the second half, I was positive I wouldn't be playing again so I still didn't put on my extra pads or change my cleats. On the first drive, though, we were on our own 28-yard line and Dennis was hit and injured again. "Shaun, go out there," the coach yelled.

I went out. They gave me the ball, and I ran hard. I was hit but stayed up. The man held on and then another man hit me. Their feet tangled, and they fell. I kept running as fast as I could and ended up with a 72-yard touchdown.

Now I had two carries, two touchdowns, and 89 yards rushing. The Alabama fans were going crazy.

Is this really happening? I asked myself. We were winning, and I was scoring touchdowns.

We stopped LSU's next drive. After they punted, I returned to the field and ran the ball on the first play, but I was hit really hard at the line of scrimmage by Anthony McFarland—and I mean *really* hard. I wasn't out of the game, though.

On second down, they threw to Shamari Buchanan, who made a diving catch at our own 26-yard line. It was third and one. The fans were holding their breath. This was the crucial moment, and everybody knew it.

John Causey, the center and team captain, looked me right in the eye. "I don't care what you do," he said, "but get this first down. We need to get a good drive going, and if we at least kick a field goal, this game's gonna be over. Alexander, we're going to make a hole for you. Even if you have to close your eyes, run—and run *hard!*"

That's exactly what I did. They handed me the ball, and I closed my eyes and ran into the hole as hard as I could. When I opened my eyes, I was at the 50-yard line heading for another touchdown.

So now I had four carries, three touchdowns, and more than 160 yards rushing. *This is unbelievable*, I kept thinking, *but it really is happening*. This was the first time I'd gotten into the "zone" in college, though it had happened often in high school. I was playing my best ever.

My twentieth carry put me over the 290 yard mark to break the school record. I finished the game with four touchdowns, 20 carries, and 291 yards—the most yards in Alabama history and one of the best rushing performances in SEC history. It was just one of those unbelievable games.

My teammates crowded around and slapped me on the back. "We're going to the championship!" "Man, you did it!" "Great game!"

"Alexander, we're gonna take you out when we get home," one of them yelled. "We're gettin' you drunk—girls—anything you want."

Chad Goss, a junior and a Christian, came up to me then. "J.D. told me you got your life verse," he said.

"Yeah, I did," I said.

"What is it?"

"Psalm 37:4."

"What does it say, Shaun?"

"It says, 'Delight yourself in the Lord and he will give you the desires of your heart.'" As soon as those words came out of my mouth, I fell silent, stunned. I realized what I had just said.

"Yeah—the Lord's real, ain't He?" Chad said and grinned knowingly.

"Oh, man, that's unbelievable." I got down on one knee right then—I didn't care who saw us or what they thought. Chad and I both prayed about God's blessings in my life. Chad's prayer was deep and full of feeling—about my being intimate with God daily. And my teammate thanked Him for showing up and showing me how powerful His Word is.

That was the first time I'd really enjoyed what I was learning from the Scripture. It was the first time I felt like I was just spending time with the Lord. And I felt as if He was saying, *Shaun, you delight in Me and I'll give you the desires of your heart.*

From that day on my faith grew, and His Word grew inside me. I expected God to do amazing things. I lived every day craving the Lord.

Chapter 8

THE OTHER COLLEGE EXPERIENCE

had been a Christian since childhood, but while I was a college student, my Christian faith was deepening and becoming a more crucial part of my life. I started thinking about my life more seriously than ever before, and I began to read the Bible more regularly.

That year, I especially remember memorizing verses two through four from the first chapter of the book of James: "Consider it pure joy, my brothers, whenever you face trials of many kinds, because you know that the testing of your faith develops perseverance. Perseverance must finish its work so that you may be mature and complete, not lacking anything."

Those verses reminded me that there are good things that can come to us through difficulties. As I repeated the words, I realized that problems and hardships strike us all. What we can do is decide how we will react. Instead of worrying about the trials and adversities, I decided I would use them like they were weights in a spiritual weight-lifting program—to make me stronger and to bring me closer to the Lord, not with tears but with dignity.

I've been blessed to do outstanding things in the game of football, but it's never been my life goal to become a gridiron star. My attitude has been, "God, You gave me this athletic ability. I'm going to set high goals for my football playing, but I'm also going to enjoy the game."

At times, my attitude has driven some of my close friends crazy. My coaches too. Even back in my peewee football days, the coaches didn't think I was serious enough. They'd tell me, "Shaun, you're not going to be able to get to the next level with that laid-back attitude."

I still laugh about that today. I think things turned out pretty well for me, after all. I think it's because underneath that seemingly lax attitude is the knowledge that this athletic ability is a gift and I'm doing the best I can with what God has given me.

With the way I look at football, Fan Day at Alabama was always a weird thing to me. All around the outside of Alabama's state-of-the-art Coleman Coliseum, tables were set up where the players would sit. Because there were a hundred-some of us, we totally circled the basketball stadium.

Fans would come in through the front door, and they would walk all the way around and stop at just about everybody's table for autographs. Fan Day certainly promoted enthusiasm for the game.

As each year went by, I was more amazed. It seemed to me that the fans grew crazier and crazier. My first year playing, they came in, talked, and asked for an autograph. Sometimes they'd ask if they could take my picture. By my sophomore year, more fans wanted their picture taken with me. I thought it was odd that boyfriends would let their girlfriends take superclose pictures where they hugged me—and would snap similar photos with other players.

One time, a young woman wanted her photo taken as she stood next to me. She put her arm around me, and the photographer prompted me, "Shaun, get closer." I moved in a little but he kept saying, "Get closer, get closer." Finally I was a little embarrassed—we were so close it probably looked like I was ready to plant a kiss on her lips. Just then he snapped the picture, and we separated. I remember asking myself, *What is wrong with these Alabama fans?* And that's when the photographer said, "Thanks, Shaun, my daughter loves you…she'll treasure this picture forever." I laughed, shook my head, and sat back down.

I realized those supporters took football to a level I had never experienced before. By the time I was a junior, they considered me a celebrity. That's when I learned a strange truth: Once you're a celebrity, people seem to want to get close. And until then, I had never linked the word *celebrity* and my name together.

By my senior year, anyone who knew anything about sports in Alabama knew who I was. I enjoyed that, but it reached the point where I couldn't walk out of the stadium without being mobbed. Some people pulled at me, and others grabbed me.

It made me feel like a rock star, and I didn't like that feeling very much. Though it was flattering, I just couldn't fit into it. After a few instances of fans coming around like that, I began to have the security guards walk me out of the stadium. For every home game, I would use a different exit. It was crazy, but I realized I was now a college football star, and all this was part of being good at the game.

◆ ❖ ◆

Each May, when the school year was over, I liked to go home and hang out with the family. But God had a different plan for me—through a man named Wayne Atcheson. I met Wayne shortly after I arrived in Alabama. He was on the university's Tide Pride staff. That was his paying job, but I knew him better as the advisor to the Alabama chapter of the Fellowship of Christian Athletes.

Everyone called Wayne "Mr. A," and I liked him immediately. He told me he had started the Alabama branch of FCA in the lobby of Bryant Hall with just four guys. Over the years, it had grown to more than a hundred athletes. Most of that was because of Mr. A's commitment and enthusiasm. He had recruited athletes from all the sports on campus to be involved. At the meetings, there was a lot of good singing, fellowship, and Bible study, and then a high-powered speaker would inspire us to be better men and women of God.

I had been going to the meetings all through my redshirt freshman and sophomore years. I liked being involved, and sometimes I'd voice my opinions about what I thought would make the meeting run smoother. Occasionally I'd suggest ways to increase our attendance.

Shortly before school ended in my second year in FCA, Mr. A asked if I'd like to go to an FCA camp. It would run June 8 through 12 in Black Mountain, North Carolina, and would take 45 college students from all over the country to be with about 450 high school kids. The huddle leaders—the college kids who were there to work with high schoolers—would check in two days earlier, on Saturday, June 6, because they needed training on how to work with the kids. On Monday, the student athletes would arrive.

"It will be an awesome camp run by college kids who love the Lord," Mr. A said. "I'd like you to be part of it, Shaun."

"I don't think I can do that," I told him. "I've decided to go home. This will be the first summer I'm not taking classes." I was looking forward to my time at home and wasn't going to let anything interfere with those plans.

But Wayne was persistent. "Shaun, I think you would really love going to Black Mountain," he said with a smile.

"I appreciate it, and I'm honored that you asked," I said, "—but I'm going to go home."

And that's exactly what I did. I went home to Kentucky and stayed there all through May and hung out with the family and friends. It was the vacation I needed.

In late May I visited one of my former coaches, Coach Paul Gray. He had been the quarterback coach at Boone County High. All of us called him P.G. Over dinner he told me he had left coaching and was considering working for FCA.

Even after the visit with P.G., I didn't think anything more about FCA or Black Mountain until a few days later, when an FCA huddle-leader coordinator called. He introduced himself as Sid Calloway from Atlanta. "I've heard many great things about you, Shaun. I'm calling because I think you'd be a great huddle leader for the FCA camp at Black Mountain."

"It's nice that you want me," I replied, "but I'm going to spend time with the family and friends. Maybe next year I'll be available."

The next day, FCA's regional director for Kentucky called. He said almost the same thing Sid Calloway had said. Again I declined.

But he kept on. "Wayne Atcheson speaks highly of you, Shaun. He thinks you'd be the best. You can be a powerful influence at this camp. It will also be good for you spiritually." When I didn't say yes, he added, "I can give you a list of some of the people who are going to be there."

"I don't think so," I repeated for the umpteenth time. "I'm enjoying time with my family right now. Maybe next year."

I thought that was the end.

I was wrong. On June 3, which was the Thursday before camp was to begin, Mr. A himself called again. "I don't want to keep bugging you, Shaun," he said, "but I feel God wants you at Black Mountain."

Before I could say no again, he asked me to pray and then call him and give him an answer.

I promised to pray about attending, but I still didn't want to go.

That night as I lay in bed, just before I went to sleep I said, "God, one more thing—if I'm supposed to go to that camp, make it really, really obvious—and I'll go."

The next morning—Friday—the phone rang. I didn't pick it up, but I listened as P.G., my former coach, left a message on the answering machine.

"Hey, Shaun—what's up?" he began. "Hey, I looked carefully at the job with FCA and I've decided to take it." He mentioned a little of what he'd be doing. Just before he hung up, he added, "On top of that, I have to go to an upcoming FCA camp in Black Mountain."

There it was again: Black Mountain.

"As I read about the camp," he went on, "I thought you'd be a great person to go with me. What do you—?"

I grabbed the phone. By then, I had gotten the message. "When do you have to go?" I asked.

"June 6. I have to be part of the leadership and help train the college kids."

"Did anybody ask you to call me?" I asked. I thought maybe Mr. A had put P.G. up to this call.

"No."

"Okay, then I'm going to go," I promised.

I hung up the phone and smiled.

"Thanks, God. You made it very clear," I said aloud.

◆ ❖ ◆

That FCA camp significantly altered my life. There I met other college kids who loved the Lord, and I enjoyed every minute with them. That camp was the beginning of my learning the meaning of accountability. I began to pick up on how much influence older men could have on younger men like me. And how I could have an influence on younger guys just coming up.

That was the first time I had been around people my age who were trying to live a life that honored God. We had some great conversations about our lifestyles and talked about how we lived as Christians in our culture and surroundings. I'd been around some of the kind of religious people who spar back and forth to see who's the smartest or knows the most about the Bible—but our conversations weren't like that.

In one such conversation someone asked me, "How far is too far to go with your girlfriend?"

I hadn't given it much thought, but I said, "I'm not sure how far is too far, but I do know that sex before marriage is wrong."

We had our Bibles with us, and two of the guys had studied what the Bible teaches about sex before marriage and sexual immorality.

> He told me, "I'm not going to kiss my wife until we're at the altar."
> "You're kidding me!" I exclaimed..."That's fine for you, but *I'm* not doing that. I *like* kissing girls."

"Sexual immorality," one of them said, "means things done sexually that God doesn't like. It's not whether *we* like it, but how God feels about it."

That had never occurred to me before—I had never thought about how God regards such things as sex. During our discussion, I also realized there was something else I hadn't thought about. In the Bible, the concept of dating wasn't mentioned.

The more we talked, the more those guys opened my eyes. As a result, I changed my attitude about dating. I wasn't then (and still am not) the kind of person who says, "Don't go out on dates." But as we talked it over and discussed the Bible, I saw how wrong my attitudes had been. It wasn't that I had been going around having sex with girls—I hadn't—but I saw what sexual immorality meant: Anything done with lustful intention is not correct in God's eyes.

There at the camp, I also met Jacob Gaydosh, a guy who became one of my good friends. He was the first person I knew who stood up boldly for sexual purity before marriage. He said one thing that absolutely astounded me. He told me, "I'm not going to kiss my wife until we're at the altar."

"You're kidding me!" I exclaimed.

"I'm serious," he said. "If we don't start on the road to intimacy, we won't finish. If we don't open the door through kissing, we don't have to struggle with how far we can go." He talked about remaining pure, and about our need to lock into what God wants, not our own desires.

"You know what?" I replied. "That's fine for you, but *I'm* not doing that. I *like* kissing girls."

We cracked up laughing.

What was great was, Jacob wasn't telling me how to live my life—he was telling me how he lived his. "That's my opinion," he summed up. "I'm not saying this means heaven or hell, but I've prayed about it, and I know this is the way God wants *me* to live."

When I went to bed that night, I thought, *I know having sex outside of marriage is wrong, but who would want to date a girl and not at least kiss her?* It didn't make sense to me.

Not then, anyway.

No one tried to pressure me, but I thought over what Jacob had said. A couple of other huddle leaders felt the same way he did—and that surprised me. They really impressed me with their love for God and their desire to get closer to Him—no matter what it took.

Over the next few days, my attitude slowly changed. I realized that no matter how I'd grown up or whatever I'd thought was right or wrong, if I went to the Bible I could set my thinking straight. I would change in the way I needed to.

That time at FCA camp started me to really consider and eventually change how I would act with girls.

◆ ❖ ◆

Each morning and evening there, a guitar player played for our worship time. We also had different speakers at night. The first was Bobby Bowden, head football coach of Florida State University. Later we had Cameron Mills, a famous basketball player from Kentucky who was on their national championship team. The last night Tony Dungy, who is now head coach of the Indianapolis Colts, spoke to us. All of these men were outstanding. The way I say it is that the whole place was "anointed"—which means that God had it marked out for something special.

One song from that week that has meant a lot to me goes like this:

> *Jesus, you're my firm foundation,*
> *I know I can stand secure.*
> *Jesus, you're my firm foundation,*
> *I put my hope in Your holy Word.* *

Those seven days changed my life. When I left, I thought, *Now I know how to lead. I understand the impact I can make.* I also knew I wanted to be part of many more FCA camps.

Looking back, I was glad God had arranged for me to be there, even though I didn't want to be at first. He made it very clear to me that I should go—and when I did, I was blessed.

During the camp I was responsible for ten kids. One who stands out is Brian Pavlick. Brian and I talked quite often during the five days he was there, and we got to know one another pretty well. And by the end of our time, every one of those ten kids, including Brian, had asked Jesus Christ to be the ruler of their lives—which is one of the things the camps emphasize.

Because of that and the rest of what I experienced, something big clicked inside my head. For the first time, I realized the importance of influence. Since I was a star athlete in college, I was able to influence boys like Brian. If I could positively affect them, they could then affect others. The domino effect could change the world. That was the beginning of a powerful concept I would later learn to put into practice.

---

* "You're My Firm Foundation," by Jamie Harvill and Nancy Gordon, ©1994 Integrity's Hosanna! Music/BMI & Integrity's Hosanna! Music/ASCAP.

And because most of the FCA camps were attended by sports teams that came in together, I had a natural bond with everybody at Black Mountain because I was a well-known football player. The leaders would bring their kids up to the camp to get extra coaching by the coaches or the college talent that was there. They would learn practical tips about playing better and also receive a strong emphasis on living like a Christian in the world.

Whenever I've done an FCA camp, one or two kids have always seemed to stand out and impact my life. At one camp, I met Cassidy, who was about 16. We hit it off from day one, when I jumped on his back and held him. "You're in my group," I told him.

He beamed when I called out, "Come on over here, cuz." It was kind of a joke, but he liked it when I called him cousin. For the rest of our time at camp, he was "cuz" to me.

As the week progressed, I learned a lot about Cassidy. He came from a strong Christian family and he already knew the Lord. I took him under my wing and told him, "I want you to become a solid man of God."

"And I will," he promised.

Another summer I went to two FCA camps. At the second, one of the kids challenged me. "I'm not going to listen to anything you say about God," he declared. "I don't want to hear that. I came to hear about football, not church."

His words really got to me. I felt like I had failed him and the others, and I needed to change my attitude. I needed to *care* about the kids I worked with. Love has to come first. I had been operating on cruise control, just teaching the kids Bible knowledge instead of focusing on their needs and on loving them. I'm thankful God taught me that at a young age. To introduce somebody to Jesus, we have to do what He did—that is, love and heal people first and foremost. So for the rest of that week, I disconnected with the outside world. I stopped calling my family and my friends. I even stopped calling my college sweetheart. Instead, I spent my free time reading the Bible and praying for the kids.

The challenge from that boy was the start of the worst experience of my FCA camps. The kids weren't as open as they had been other times. *But then,* I thought, *maybe I haven't been open to them.*

Over the coming days, their attitudes changed toward me because my attitude changed first. I learned to care about them.

And the boy who didn't want to hear about God? On the last night, he asked Jesus Christ take over his life.

I threw myself into helping the kids at every FCA camp I attended. I determined to love them twice as hard. I started praying with some of them. I made sure I gave all of them individual attention.

I promised myself I'd never go to another FCA camp without being focused and open with the kids.

I've kept that promise.

Chapter 9

SENIOR YEAR

Vanderbilt was the first game on the schedule of my senior season. Just before we were to leave I came down with a high temperature. I ached everywhere. I felt dizzy and nauseated, and had diarrhea. I couldn't remember ever feeling so sick. The team doctor was ready to shoot medicine down my throat so I could get on the bus to Nashville. I vaguely recall reaching the stadium and the outside temperature being more than a hundred degrees.

Sick or not, I played. When I sat on the bench, my body shook with chills, and then I'd overheat. The score was going back and forth, and as bad as I felt, I went back in at the end of the fourth quarter and made a big play. All I can remember is that I caught a long pass for a touchdown and had more than 100 yards rushing. I have to add that Vanderbilt wasn't really that good a team and that helped us to win.

After the game, the media people jumped on my case. "Didn't you attend spring practice?" they asked. "You really looked out of shape."

After a few more such questions, Coach Mike DuBose answered for me. "It's probably the 101-degree temperature he has."

"Really?" one of them asked.

"This boy is sick, and he still played," Coach DuBose explained.

That was a very good start for my senior year of football. Even though I was sick, I still had a great game.

We played our second game against Houston, and I scored three touchdowns again, as I had in the Vanderbilt game. Our third game was with Louisiana Tech—a home game for us. I had two touchdowns and ran a kickoff back for my third touchdown. It was a great game. Tim Rattay, their star quarterback, was good. (He later went on to play for the 49ers.) But he was injured on the next-to-last play of the game, so they brought in their backup. He threw a 30- or 40-yard pass to the sideline, which was caught. The receiver stepped out of bounds to stop the clock—and then the quarterback threw a 28-yard touchdown pass with five seconds left. With that touchdown catch, we lost the game—and, in my mind, a shot at winning the national championship that season. I thought it was our most embarrassing loss ever because it was so freakish. But then, sometimes games are like that.

The next week we played Arkansas. It was the worst game of my senior year—I had a bunch of fumbles. Andrew Zow, our star quarterback, had a number of interceptions. As badly as we played, I don't know how we won that game. But we did—barely. I scored one touchdown and gained 182 yards. It was still a bad game—I knew it, and I think we all knew it.

The year before, Coach DuBose had pulled aside several of the guys and told them about an affair he'd had—and ended—with a woman at the office. He'd said, "This is what happened. I told my wife, we fixed it up. I've given myself to the Lord. I've repented, and I'm back in focus again, but I want you guys to know about it so you can pay attention to your mistakes."

I thought that was a really humbling experience to keep on teaching in the midst of that. We were now facing our next game—against the Florida

Gators—and rumor had it that the university was going to fire Coach DuBose over the affair.

That wasn't right. Yes, he had done wrong. But he had confessed it, and his wife had forgiven him. Shouldn't that have been the end of it? Why were people treating him like that?

Adultery is sin, but so is not being willing to forgive.

You can understand why the team might have felt motivated about the Florida game. And something else happened the week before the game that gave me a real boost. I passed the office where Coach Williams, my running back coach, sat at his desk, talking on the phone. His back was to me, and just before I spoke up, I heard him say, "Alexander? Oh, yeah, he's ready and he's gonna kill them."

That was the first time I'd ever heard Coach Williams speak about me with such confidence. His words made me feel great. *I'm the man*, I thought, *and I'm going to show it.*

Our relationship had developed to where I could talk to Coach Williams like a good friend, so when he said I was "gonna kill them," I knew how he really felt about me and my ability. He couldn't have said anything more powerful or encouraging. Best of all, I'd overheard him saying it to someone else.

There's something special when a father or a man of authority speaks highly about his kid or his player. And Coach Williams wasn't just boasting. The tone of his voice convinced me of his sincerity.

During the days that followed I felt wonderful. I was in the frame of mind that I was going to take the whole game onto my shoulders. I was going to be *the man* to win the game against the Florida Gators in the Swamp, which is what they called their stadium. I would be the one to end their six-year winning streak at home. Even though the Gators had won their last 30 games in a row and were ranked number three in the nation, I didn't feel anxious. Coach Williams's words had put confidence deep in my heart.

◆ ❖ ◆

Wednesday, when we finished our practice, an alum came up to me and said, "You know, Shaun, you and the boys play hard. And no matter what happens we're going to be proud of you." It was obvious he was trying to console us in advance for a loss.

I stared at him for a few seconds. "Did you forget we're Alabama?"

"Well, of course not—"

"And we're going to win," I continued. "And when this game is over, you need to apologize to me and my team."

Some of the other guys heard me. And when one person gets passionate about something and shows confidence, it can ignite an entire team. That was what was happening.

We jumped on the plane that Friday night, flew into Gainesville, Florida, and rested up. The next day while we dressed, I became aware of how quiet it was. Usually there was a lot of talking and laughing, but I sensed an electric energy over the entire locker room. We *knew* we were going to beat the Gators.

> Coach DuBose walked into the locker room, smiled, chuckled, and said, "I want everyone to remember this moment. No one but us knows what we're about to do to Florida."

Coach DuBose walked into the locker room, smiled, chuckled, and said, "I want everyone to remember this moment. No one but us knows what we're about to do to Florida."

"Yeah!" came the first voice.

And a lot of raucous laughter followed.

"We're gonna do it!" one of the guys yelled.

We went out on the field, and the fight began. I scored a touchdown early in the second quarter. Then they threw a deep pass to their star receiver, Darrell Jackson, for a Gator touchdown.

At halftime, Alabama was ahead 13–7, but in the second quarter I'd gone for a pass across the middle, and two guys had hit me and knocked off my helmet. My mouth was busted and my nose was cut, but I wasn't out of the game.

The second half was action-packed. The Gators threw another pass to Darrell for his third touchdown, which put them up by seven pretty near the end of the fourth quarter. The score was 33–26, and it didn't look good for us.

They stopped us on the next drive. When we punted, Darrell was actually the returner, but he fumbled. One of their guys jumped on it. Our guys jumped on top of him, and everybody fought under the pile.

Two of our sophomores were at the bottom of the pile fighting with one of the Florida guys. They later said all they could remember was that they were not going to let us lose. They punched at the football, punched at the guy under the pile, pulled on his helmet, grabbed his throat, and yanked at the ball. When they pulled everyone off, our backup fullback, Marvin Brown, held the ball.

"Look at that!" someone yelled from the stands. All of us jumped up and down and screamed. We had possession of the ball and we drove hard down the field. After we made a couple of passes I got the ball with about a minute left in the game. I broke a tackle and ran for a touchdown. That, with the extra point, tied the score 33–33, and we went into overtime.

In college football overtime, both teams get the ball at the 25-yard line to see who can score the most points. If both score even, they do the same thing again.

As overtime began, Florida got the ball first, and they scored. They tried to kick the extra point, and their kicker missed it. The score was 39–33.

I jumped up and down in excitement and ran over to Coach Williams. "Run the counter!" I said.

"That's a great idea," he said. He called in on his headset: "Shaun likes the counter."

We huddled up at the sideline, and Andrew, the quarterback, ran in to join us. "All right, ya'll—this is it," he said. He called the counter play to the left.

It felt like slow motion to me. I acted as if I was going to the right, cut back over to the left, and they gave me the ball. I saw one block, got past it, and then a second. I jumped out of the hole. Ahead of me, one of our tight ends, Shawn Draper, slammed one of their guys to the ground at the ten-yard line. After I passed Shawn, I realized something—no one was in front of me. I crossed the goal line and scored on our first play in overtime.

That score tied us at 39–39. Our extra point team ran out on the field and snapped the ball, Chris Kemp, our backup field goal kicker, put it up…and missed.

"There's a flag on the field!" someone yelled. That meant we were going to have another chance to kick. Later, I learned that Florida had jumped offside and our center had snapped it early so that we'd get the flag. Chris tried the kick again—and made it!

We had beaten Florida 40–39 in overtime, breaking their 30-game win streak and their six-year streak of home wins.

Impulsively I jumped into Coach Williams's arms, and he danced a jig. Totally jazzed, I jumped up on the bleachers and cheered with the 'Bama fans.

We celebrated, screamed, and yelled. I also believe that win meant we had saved Coach DuBose's job.

On Monday that alum *did* come back to apologize to us.

◆ ❖ ◆

Before the next game, we had a bye week, so we were able to rest up. I was able to go home and see my friends Ray and Brian play during their the senior night game for Western Kentucky against Eastern Kentucky. Their team won.

Our next game was against Ole Miss. I had one of my best college games that day, with 214 yards rushing and three touchdowns.

We played Tennessee next, which turned out to be a significant game for me—but not for good reasons. I was hurt in the beginning of the fourth quarter after gaining 98 yards rushing with a touchdown. Because of the high-ankle sprain I suffered, I played very little in the next two games.

After that was the Auburn game.

◆ ❖ ◆

In Alabama, there's no bigger game for a senior than the one against Auburn. The big week started off badly, though. When Mike Gurley and I were driving back to school from his home, we hit a deer. We were fine—however, there was a big dent in one of the doors of my Ford Explorer. We were able to drive on to the Ford dealership in Tuscaloosa, but because it was closed, we left the car there with a note on the windshield saying we were leaving for Auburn and would pick it up when we returned. I didn't give any details—I didn't want anyone to know about the accident. I had just come off the injured list from the ankle sprain and didn't want anyone to mistakenly think I might be hurt again.

That all sounds pretty serious, but there was a funny side to the story.

Mike had been driving when I heard him ask all of a sudden, "Hey, is that a deer up ahead?"

It was standing right in the middle of the road. We slowed down, it leaped past us—but then it turned around, and its head hit the back door of the Explorer. It spun around and fell.

Mike pulled to the side, and we jumped out and looked over the damage. I don't know how to judge a deer, but this one was big—it had a lot of points.

A man pulled up behind us. "Hey, you kids all right?"

"Yeah," I said.

"I'm going to get some help," he said and drove off.

Just then another car pulled up.

"Hey, are both of you all right?"

"Yeah, we're okay," I said.

"Somebody already went to get help," Mike added.

The guy glanced around. "Can I have the deer?" he asked.

"Sure," I said. "Take it."

"Now we know we're in Alabama," Mike quipped, and we had a good laugh.

We ended up having a great game against Auburn, and we won. I scored three touchdowns and rushed for 182 yards.

Two weeks later, the dealer had repaired my car. I picked it up, and no one ever knew about it.

It was during my senior year that Alabama decided to launch their first-ever Heisman campaign. The Heisman Trophy is given annually to the top college player and is the most prestigious award in college football. Alabama had never pushed an athlete for the Heisman, even though they've had many great players. That year they decided to push me.

But having missed those three games because of the ankle injury cost me my chance at the Heisman. That was a disappointment, of course, but I was so thrilled to be back playing again, I didn't feel too bad. I have said this several times: "We all set goals and sometimes barely miss them. Don't be depressed. Instead, be thankful for where you are. Use the near misses as fuel for later success." By that I'm referring to the tough times and events that appear to be failures. My failures are often the things in life that have pushed me to be better and stronger.

Yes, winning the Heisman would have been nice. I would have loved the honor—but I didn't get it, and I understood. I figure I would probably have earned it if I hadn't been hurt, but injuries are a part of football.

Some people may not understand that attitude, but I had prayed for God's will in the matter of the Heisman. I had done my best.

I was—and still am—content to say, "Thank You, God, for what You give me."

Something else really important for me happened during my senior year at Alabama. My friend Ronnie Cottrell and I had often spoken about the bigger issues in life. I'd said to him that when I was in a position to do so, I'd like to help kids and needy families. I told him of my dreams of mentoring kids and offering scholarships to help them get an education.

Ronnie said, "That's good, Shaun—but you don't have to wait to do it."

"What do you mean?" I asked.

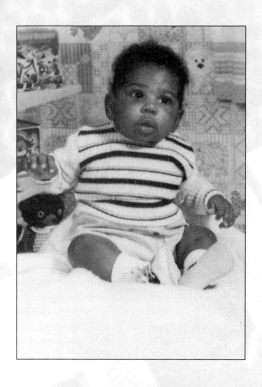

1977, enjoying my first year of a blessed life.

The Alexander family: Dad (Curtis), Mom (Carol), Durran, and me.

My elder brother (by one year) Durran and me dressed in our Sunday best.

Here's my 3rd grade photo.

Durran and me—peewee football stars!

The Alexander brothers at ages 10 and 9.

The budding running back at age 11.

Boone County High School running back. Finally got my number…37.

Looking dapper for my junior prom.

Having a great night at my senior prom. Here I am with Ben Brown and Josh Hays.

Sitting in front of the legendary high school football coach, Owen Hauck, as we announce that I will attend the University of Alabama.

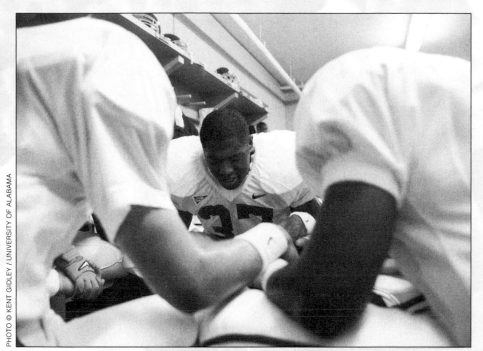

Before each game, some of us would pray together.

During Fan Day, the players line the gym and sign autographs for our fans.

Here I am carrying the ball during our game against the Arkansas Razorbacks on September 25, 1999. We won 35–28. I had 165 yards on 34 carries and 1 touchdown.

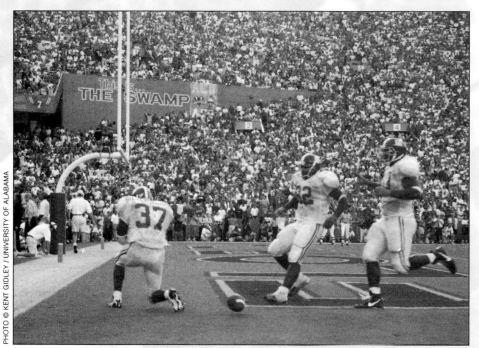

Here I am scoring a TD against Florida, October 2, 1999. Our win (40–39) broke their six-year winning streak at The Swamp.

Greeting fans after our victory. "Roll, Tide!"

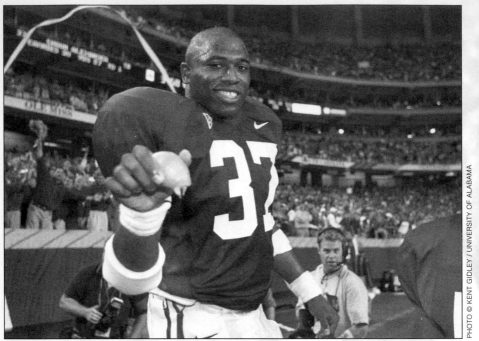

December 4, 1999. This was the day we won the SEC championship and a ticket to the Orange Bowl by beating Florida 34–7.

I love the Fellowship of Christian Athletes. It's a great organization, and I've spoken many times on behalf of FCA. This was at an FCA Orange Bowl breakfast in Miami.

Here I am participating in my NFL private workout during Pro Day in the year 2000.

Durran and Mom at my graduation from the University of Alabama.

This was the day (April 14, 2000) I was honored at the Denny Chimes bell tower as a captain of the Crimson Tide. At the base of the tower is the Alabama football Captains' Walk of Fame, which bears hand and foot impressions of each captain from Crimson Tide teams dating back to the 1940s.

Hugs all around as the announcement is made: "For pick number 19, the Seattle Seahawks choose Shaun Alexander from Alabama." My agent had caps from several teams on hand…just in case. And one of those was a Seahawks cap, which I put on right after the good news was broadcast.

Durran and I broke ground on the Alexander Community Center in Florence, Kentucky, in the summer of 2005. The building used to be a YMCA and is being renovated to become a top-of-the-line facility available to all ages, races, income levels, and athletic abilities.

Here I am running the game ball out in Alabama's annual Iron Bowl matchup against our rival, Auburn, during my bye week of my rookie year in the NFL.

Durran—still my best counselor—and his daughter, my beautiful niece, Maleah, in Hawaii for the Pro Bowl, 2006.

With Valerie in Hawaii, 2006.

Receiving the MVP Award was a special occasion for me. Here I am, surrounded by some of the Seahawks coaching staff, including Coach Mike Holmgren to my left.

Receiving a handoff from Matt Hasselbeck.

I knew Ronnie often went to various churches and talked to them about helping poor kids. "You could do that too, Shaun," he explained. "You have the same passion for helping others." He told me about Choctaw County, the poorest county in Alabama, and challenged me to begin *now*—not someday in the future—to help raise scholarship funds for needy kids.

His admonition was the beginning of what would later become the Shaun Alexander Foundation. I started it while I was still in Alabama, hoping I'd go on to play professional football. If I did, I'd be ready. Ronnie helped me see that I didn't have to have millions of dollars before I started helping kids. Start where you are, was his message. Start with what you have, not with what you may someday have.

Ronnie helped me arrange speaking opportunities. We also began to set up events to raise money. One of the first was a golf tournament to raise scholarship funds to help a student go to college. We asked the kids who applied for the scholarship to have at least a B average and good school attendance. The event went well, and we brought in enough to endow a scholarship to the University of Alabama for one Choctaw County student.

"This is only the first one," Ronnie told me.

And he was right. What is today the Shaun Alexander Foundation simply grew from my conversations with Ronnie.

◆ ❖ ◆

After the golf tournament, I spent much of my free time during the following months raising money to help needy kids.

At the time of the Orange Bowl game against Michigan, I had recently been a candidate for the Heisman, and that brought me a lot of nationwide attention. The publicity sparked more invitations to speak...and when I spoke it was a way for me to talk about meeting the needs of kids.

> We were still new at this, and we didn't know what we were doing. We rented an entire building.

On February 1, 2000, a month after the Orange Bowl, we officially started the Shaun Alexander Foundation. We planned for our first event to be held in Tuscaloosa in July.

Like anyone undertaking such a project, I needed help. Durran had received his degree in marketing from Notre Dame, and I was soon to receive mine from Alabama. I wanted him to work with me in my foundation. I wanted him at my side. He was a person I could trust for anything. He would be my eyes and ears in business matters, and he'd pay attention in places where I didn't.

At that time, Durran worked at the Campbell Soup Company. He was the youngest sales rep in their history. So I called him up. "How much do you get paid in your job?" I asked.

When he told me, I said, "I'll match it."

By then, both of us were pretty sure I'd be a first-round draft choice, so money shouldn't be a problem.

Durran took the jump. He quit his job and came to work for the foundation, helping me set it up right. Initially I paid his salary because we didn't have any money in the organization. Even so, it was a leap of faith for him. After all, I hadn't yet been drafted by the NFL.

We talked to many people to learn everything we could. We wanted to do this right. That first event in Tuscaloosa was to be a dinner on Friday night, July 7, 2000. Though we had a number of cool things going on, we were still new at this, and we didn't know what we were doing.

We rented an entire building. We had decorated tables everywhere and were set up for thousands of people—we were that pumped. But in the end, I think somewhere between 300 and 400 people actually showed up. They were a great crowd, but not the thousands we had hoped and planned for. We sure learned a lot from that experience, though. And despite the smaller crowd than we'd expected, we paid our expenses and had a little money to put into the foundation. It was a success despite our overplanning.

After that, we set up a Thanksgiving dinner, which we followed with a big Christmas dinner for the homeless in Tuscaloosa. It was even bigger than the Thanksgiving event. Even though by then I had moved away from that part of the country, a number of the Alabama players showed up to help pass out food and toys. I was proud of the team for showing up. It was just two days before Christmas—they could have said, "No, it's December, and I'm going to relax and just hang out."

That night, Andrew Zow, then Alabama's star quarterback, was passing out toys and food to a woman with three children. He asked her if he could also pray for her, but she surprised him by saying, "No, please let me pray for *you.*"

Andrew again offered to pray for her. That's why he was there—to help and encourage her. But she repeated, "No, I'd really like to pray for you. I *need* to pray for you." And she gave Andrew the only thing she had to give—her prayers.

When I heard that story, it was such a blessing to me and a strong lesson for all of us. When we think we're doing great things for other people, we have to realize how much *they* really have to offer *us.*

That was such an awesome lesson.

◆ ❖ ◆

In my first year of football after college, I didn't have much playing time. I was able to use my time to think of ways to bring money to the foundation. We realized that although we could do events, the biggest way to bring in money was for me to go out and speak. And that's what I did.

I began to speak whenever and wherever I could. I spoke to many churches in Kentucky, where I was already known. In Alabama, I was able to speak to some leaders of corporations and urge them to do more for their community.

These corporations would then ask me to speak at their events. And when I did so, I'd tell them about the foundation and what we were trying to do, and I'd ask them to make a donation.

They always said yes.

Later, wider doors opened. As my career ramped up, I was getting invitations to play in golf tournaments and was able to meet some celebrities who were also willing to help support the foundation.

Durran and I thought about doing another golf tournament, but then he said, "You know, everyone has a golf tournament. Why don't we do something different?"

After talking over a number of possibilities, we came up with the idea of a celebrity softball game. We set it up at the Hank Aaron Stadium in Mobile. We had an excellent turnout and great participation, which helped raise money for our Christmas and Thanksgiving events.

I'll always remember that first softball event. I hit four home runs! That *must* have been God smiling on me!

Later on, the Shaun Alexander Foundation grew and changed, but those first years were special. I think of how inexperienced Durran and I were and how much we had to learn. I also think about how much fun we had and how much we saw God do through us.

I can only come to one conclusion: That also must have been God smiling on us.

Chapter 10

DRAFT CHOICE

Around the world, the arrival of the year 2000 brought all sorts of celebrations. And in my life, the opening months of that year were packed with events that would have a long-term effect on me.

On New Year's Day I played my last game as part of the Crimson Tide at the Orange Bowl in Miami against Michigan. The next day I was to meet with three agents who wanted to represent me when I turned pro.

I met two of them at a hotel in Miami. After they left, I talked with the third, Richard Katz, who I'd known since I was a boy. Among the other players he represented was John Jackson, who was from my own area and had played with the Pittsburgh Steelers.

I wanted to pick the right agent, and it had to be somebody I felt I could trust. The first agent I met with was a strong Christian, and I had heard a lot of good things about him. He had all the qualities I liked, but somehow our personalities just didn't fit well together. The second man seemed like a fine agent too, but again, I wasn't totally comfortable with him, so I decided he wasn't the one.

I went back to Richie Katz. Even though he didn't represent a first-rounder or a superstar such as a running back or quarterback, I felt I could trust him. I sensed he would do the best for me that he knew how. And John Jackson, his client, had just signed the highest lineman contract in history. That impressed me.

Richie was my guy.

I was ready for the NFL draft.

◆ ❖ ◆

Each year just before the draft process, there's an event held in Indianapolis called the Pro Combine, where the top college players are invited to go through some rigorous workouts and tests for NFL scouts in hopes of improving their chances in the upcoming draft. This year the event was held in late February.

The NFL Draft

Before the actual draft picks, which happen in April, the National Football League has one big event in Indianapolis, the Pro Combine. There NFL coaches and scouts invite the best college players in the country to work out for them—sort of like an audition. Players get physicals, take mental tests, and do workouts such as run 40-yard sprints and bench press 225 pounds as many times as they can.

Some of the players decide not to work out at the Pro Combine, but instead let the scouts and coaches see them work out at their own colleges. That doesn't happen with a lot of players, but there are always a few.

Then, in April, the owners of the teams meet in New York's Madison Square Garden, and all 32 teams try to grab the best players coming out of college.

To make it as even as possible, the team with the worst record from the previous year picks first, thus ensuring them the best shot at the top player in the draft. The reigning Super Bowl team picks last. After all 32 teams have picked once, the second round begins with the same rules. However—and here is where it can be complicated—teams may trade players or picks to change their position in the selection process. This often makes for a busy, hectic day of wheeling and dealing.

It's not uncommon for many of the top athletes to not train at this event. They often want to wait and train at their own home stadium…and that's what I decided to do.

My reason was to give me more time for preparation. I had a great Olympic sprint coach, Joe Gentry, who I knew would help me get ready.

The opportunity to be observed by NFL coaches and scouts is crucial because those who don't perform well could lose millions of dollars.

A month or so after the Pro Combine, NFL scouts visited the University of Alabama and watched me work out. I knew I was in good shape. I knew I was ready, but the irony still haunted me as I thought: *All the work we do in high school and college, and it can be destroyed by one bad workout day.*

◆ ❖ ◆

In February, I was alerted to the next big event in my life when I got a call from Durran. Florence, Kentucky, was naming a street after me. It would be called Shaun Alexander Way—it's the street that leads into the Boone County High School campus next to the tennis courts.

The ceremony was on March 2, and it was a great privilege for me to be honored in this way in my own hometown.

But just several days later, another interesting turn of events happened in my life when I was visiting my cousin Michael Story, who's a pastor. He's about 15 years older than I am, a great friend, and someone whose wisdom I've depended on through the years.

During my visit, when Michael was out of the room, his wife, Vicki, turned to me and said, "Shaun...I'm not sure I should tell you this, but..."

"Tell me what?" I asked.

She hesitated a moment, then said, "Shaun, I believe God has a wife for you, and I believe she's right around the corner."

"Really—that's cool," I said. "Which corner?"

We both laughed, but I knew what she meant. I was 22 and had been hoping I might meet my wife soon. Still, this wasn't the kind of thing I expected to hear from Vicki, so I took her words seriously.

Minutes later Michael came back into the room. He put his hand on my shoulder and said, "I'm really proud of you, Shaun. You're getting ready for the draft and a great career. It must be a great feeling."

"It sure is," I said.

"But there's something else," he continued. "I'm not sure I should tell you this...but..."

"But what?"

"Shaun, I have a strong feeling your wife is right around the corner."

I looked at Vicki.

She shook her head in amazement and said, "Michael, I just told Shaun the exact same thing!"

He laughed and said, "That's amazing. You know, God is good. Pay attention now, Shaun."

I said I sure would. Then just a little later, Michael said something else that stirred my faith: "Shaun, no matter what happens with this draft, I want you to know God has the perfect plan for you. Don't worry about what's going on or what happens. God will put you exactly where He needs you. You've just got to believe it."

His words would prove to be true. And I *did* believe it. I still do.

When I graduated in 2000, I knew of five NFL teams that wanted running backs: the Baltimore Ravens, the Arizona Cardinals, the New York Giants, the Detroit Lions, and the Kansas City Chiefs.

The Cincinnati Bengals, who were attractive to me because Cincinnati was close to my hometown, had the fourth draft pick. However, they already had a good running back in Corey Dillon, who was from Seattle. Still, a rumor was circulating that they might trade him to Seattle and end up picking me.

The draft was to take place on April 15, 2000. The day before I was at Alabama for a very important ceremony. To be honest, I was more excited about that than I was about the NFL draft.

Alabama has a long tradition of putting the handprints and footprints of the captains of their football team in cement. They call the spot where they do it the Captains' Walk. I was captain in 1999/2000, so my prints would be on that walk.

Someone pointed out how many great NFL players had once played for the Crimson Tide—Joe Namath, Ken Stabler, Leroy Jordon, Tony Nathan, Jeremiah Castille, Derrick Thomas, and others. I felt honored to have my handprints and footprints alongside theirs.

I went to sleep that night after the ceremony and woke up the morning of April 15 to fly home to Kentucky. Everything was done first-class. It was a new experience for me to be treated so well. A limousine picked me up from the airport, and the chauffeur drove me past Shaun Alexander Way.

We had barely arrived in Florence when I received a call from the Arizona Cardinals. The owner said, "Shaun, we've got the seventh pick, and if you're still not chosen by then, we want to pick you. However, we know the Ravens might have already chosen you by then." The Baltimore Ravens had the fifth pick, and the Bengals—perhaps also interested—had the fourth pick, as I mentioned. Plus, I had also heard from my agent that the New York Giants, who had the eleventh pick, might be interested, so it seemed that I would surely be among the first dozen picks in the first round.

My church friends, especially the Sellers, along with others that I considered part of my extended family in Alabama, agreed to attend my personal party that evening, when the draft picks would be televised. My agent, Richie Katz, had set it up at the Montgomery Boathouse, a beautiful restaurant that looks out over the Ohio River.

When I arrived at the restaurant, more than 200 people were there. As soon as I was sure I had greeted everyone, yet another hand reached out to shake mine. I have no idea how many people brought cameras, but they seemed to be everywhere.

One special guest was my friend, Haley Hunt, who is also my sister-in-law. She had written a song called "He's on Fire," and she played a CD with the song on it. That was one of the sweetest moments of the day. I still have that CD and often enjoy listening to it.

Although there was a lot of food and people kept offering to get me a plate, I just couldn't eat much. Part of the reason was the excitement, but also people kept talking to me and shaking hands—and I really had no chance to eat.

When the draft started, everyone quieted down, and we all gathered at the tables to watch the telecast. The first choice, by the Cleveland Browns, was Courtney Brown of Penn State. The second choice, given to the Redskins, was LaVar Arrington, also from Penn State. Chris Samuels, one of the best offensive linemen in Alabama college team history, went third. I liked him and felt excited for him.

"Here's the fourth pick!" someone yelled. "It's the Bengals."

When their pick was announced, it turned out to be a buddy of mine, Peter Warrick, who played for Florida State. We had played together at Alabama, and he was an excellent choice. Some of my friends were upset, but I wasn't. I hadn't really expected the Bengals to draft me. I figured I'd go on the seventh pick, so I waited. Fifth pick was the Baltimore Ravens, and I hoped they'd take me. Maybe it was the money—or perhaps it was because they were closer to Kentucky.

The order in which a player is picked is important. The lower the number, the higher the pay scale. More than that, it also means the player receives more up-front money. It's easy for the top choices to get ten million dollars. Of course, the higher the number, the lower the pay scale. (Believe me, none of it is bad.)

> I remembered my cousin Michael's words—that God had a perfect plan for me. So I tried to focus on that, and not on the teams that weren't picking me.

"The fifth pick," the announcer said, "by Baltimore, is Jamal Lewis from the University of Tennessee." I knew and liked Jamal. And I could honestly clap for him. I would have liked to be picked by the Ravens, but I was happy for Jamal.

The sixth pick raced past me because I was waiting for the seventh—by the Arizona Cardinals. I was thinking I might as well get ready to go to Arizona because it seemed like that was where I'd be playing.

One thing bothered me a little, though—I hadn't received any further phone calls. Usually, the teams call the players a few minutes before the pick.

For the seventh pick, Arizona chose Thomas Jones from Virginia.

"*What?*" screamed my Uncle Albert. "They picked the wrong guy!"

I didn't say anything, but I was shocked. And yes, I felt disappointed. Then I remembered my cousin Michael's words—that God had a perfect plan for me. So I tried to focus on that, and not on the teams that weren't picking me.

Earlier in the week, I had talked to several professional players and they'd urged me not to watch the draft process. "You get caught up in the whole thing," they told me, "then you end up not being one of the first guys who gets picked and you hate yourself." Now, for a few seconds I wondered, *Is that going to happen to me?* I pushed away that thought because, following no mention of my name at the eighth, ninth, and tenth picks, the New York Giants now had the eleventh pick. Everyone, I'm told, wants to play in the Big Apple. I decided I'd like that.

The Giants were going to pick a running back—we knew that. And then they announced it. "The eleventh pick is Heisman Trophy winner Ron Dayne from Virginia."

"Oh, no!" someone near me cried out.

"Are they *crazy?*" someone else exclaimed.

What's going on here? I kept asking myself. Again I felt rejected. I had really expected the Giants to pick me.

By now I saw that some of my friends were amazed and disappointed at my not being chosen in the first dozen picks. A few were angry.

Durran turned to me. "Are you all right?" he asked.

"They just messed with my money right there," I said. That brought a laugh and broke the tension in the room.

Then came the twelfth pick, followed by the thirteenth through fifteenth. Those teams needed mostly defensive players, so I didn't think much about not getting picked by them.

Then, for the sixteenth pick—halfway through the first round—the San Francisco 49ers chose Julian Peterson from Michigan State.

At that point my cousin Michael came up and put his arm around me. "I don't understand why you look worried, Shaun." He went on to remind me of what he'd said just a few days before.

His words brought me back to reality. *There are things much bigger than the draft,* I told myself. *Even if I don't get picked in the first round, that's going to be all right.* After all, there are lots of players to choose from. There are 119 Division One colleges. There's also Division One AA, Division Two, and Division Three. Just to be in the draft is an honor. Being picked is special—being picked in the first three rounds is more than special—and being picked in the first round is absolutely the best. But it can't happen to everyone.

Just before the pick by the 49ers, a Seattle Seahawks representative had called me and said, "We have the nineteenth pick—has anybody called you yet?"

Before I could answer, he'd said, "Shaun, we hope to get you. If no one grabs you first, we want you."

Minutes later, I heard the announcement: "For pick number 19, the Seattle Seahawks choose Shaun Alexander from Alabama."

I couldn't believe the noise from my friends and relatives—all the cheering and the shouting.

I smiled. I hadn't particularly wanted to go to Seattle, but now that it was a reality, I was fine with it. I began to grin then—and once I started, I couldn't stop.

God wanted me in Seattle, of all places.

◆ ❖ ◆

The owner of the Seahawks is Paul Allen, a former partner of Microsoft's Bill Gates. Paul built Seattle's version of the Rock 'n' Roll Hall of Fame, the EMP—Experience Music Project. He also owns the Portland Trail Blazers basketball team.

On April 16, the day after the draft, I flew to Seattle. I met Coach Mike Holmgren shortly after I arrived. We shook hands, and I thanked him for choosing me.

"Shaun, we're expecting great things from you," he told me.

Maybe he said that to every new player. It didn't matter—he had said the words to me. *That mattered.*

Even when I first arrived in Seattle, I thought Mike Holmgren was the best coach in the NFL. Earlier, he had led the Green Bay Packers to the Super Bowl. And now, looking back over my years with the team, I'm even more convinced he's the best. He's not only a man of enormous confidence, but he instills that same confidence in the rest of us.

Coach Holmgren is my kind of guy. Like all coaches and players, we've had a few bad moments—that's part of the sport. But when it comes to offense, he's one of the smartest coaches I've been around. There are plays that—when we run them—it almost looks as if the defense isn't there on the field. That's because Mike sets them up so perfectly. When our receivers can run wide open down the field on pass plays and make the catches, it's because Coach Holmgren has planned the plays so well. I'd never been around an offense like that till I joined the Seahawks.

That first day in Seattle, I thought about how my life was turning out and was amazed at all that had happened, particularly with coaches. I'd had one of the best high school coaches in Kentucky history. I'd gone to Alabama where Gene Stallings had coached—one of the best coaches in their history. Now I stood in front of Mike Holmgren, another great coach. It seems that all my life I've been surrounded by great coaches.

Now that I was in the NFL, I was facing some big adjustments. Being drafted meant I had to deal with a whole different level of celebrity than what I'd been used to as a player for Alabama. Adding to it was the fact that in May I received the award for the Southeastern Conference Male Athlete of the Year.

Everybody's expectations of me changed. Now more than ever, people wanted me to come and speak to them. Others figured I probably wouldn't be available anymore.

When I later flew to Bristol, Tennessee, to attend my fourth FCA camp, I had barely gotten there when one of the kids ran up to me.

"You're here! You're really here!"

"Sure I am," I said.

"But you're a pro now!"

"That's right."

"And you're still doing FCA camps?"

Others had the same question. Why would I bother to come there when I had turned professional?

"Because helping kids is a part of who I am," I told them. "This is where I can come to help those kids turn on to God."

Nothing had changed regarding my concern for kids in need.

It still hasn't.

I credit God with helping me deal with all the fame and celebrity. Some other guys had big attitude problems to deal with. They also had a tough time moving to a new place and adjusting to their new role as a pro. But when I flew back to Seattle to begin settling in, I was able to take it as, "Well, this is the next step in God's plan. Good things are going to happen." I could agree completely with what my cousin Michael reminded me of at the draft party: "Shaun, I *told* you God has everything perfectly planned out for you. So you can smile. God knows what He's doing, right?"

Right.

Chapter 11

THE GIRL IN THE
LITTLE GREEN NEON

returned to Seattle on Thursday, May 25. At that time I knew only one of the Seahawks players, Kendrick Burton, who had been a senior at Alabama when I was a freshman. When I had first arrived at Alabama, Kendrick and I and some of the older guys had gone fishing together, although seniors didn't usually hang out with the lowly freshmen. During that outing, he'd told me, "Shaun, I'm going to take care of you. If you ever need anything, you come find me." Five years later, I would take him up on his promise.

It was evening when I landed in Seattle. On Friday Kendrick had invited a number of people to come over to his apartment to watch the L.A. Lakers play the Portland Trail Blazers, so one of his friends on the team picked me up from the hotel to take me over there. During the drive, he started telling me about Kendrick's girlfriend, Cindi. She played basketball and was a power forward for Seattle Pacific University. Then he mentioned her roommate, Valerie Boyd, one of the backup point guards.

After we arrived at his apartment, Kendrick greeted me and we began talking. After a few minutes he said, "You know, you need to meet my girlfriend's roommate, Valerie. She's funny, spunky, very good-looking, loves the Lord. You'll get along really well with her."

"That's cool," I responded politely but without a lot of interest. Other people's ideas of what I might want in a girl were usually different from mine. It did make me prick up my ears, though, when Kendrick added one more thing about Valerie: "She's keeping herself pure."

Although there were only about eight people at the party when I first walked through the door, others began walking in fairly quickly. One of the arrivals was a pretty girl wearing a miniskirt, and I was hoping she wasn't Valerie.

Everyone gathered around the TV as the game came on, eating and talking. I was sitting near the window and happened to look out just as a little green Neon pulled up and a really beautiful young woman stepped out. Immediately I thought, *I'd like to go outside and find out who* that *girl is.* But I wasn't going to do anything like introduce myself to just any girl on the street.

I kept watching the game, listening to bits of conversations around me—and then, the girl I'd seen in the green Neon walked in the front door. As I spotted her, one of the young women from Seattle Pacific turned and greeted her with the words, "Hey, Valerie, how you doing?"

So *that* was Valerie? Yes, I decided—I would like to meet her.

The two women talked a little, and the first one asked Valerie the question I wanted to hear: "Valerie, do you know Shaun? He's—"

"Valerie!" I interrupted. "Didn't we fly to New York together?"

"New York?" she asked blankly.

"Right! And you know, I haven't seen you since that trip," I said. "How are you doing?"

Valerie stared at me a moment longer before she caught on to my joke. "Oh, I'm doing good," she said. "And New York was fun. How about you?"

"You guys already know each other?" her friend asked.

We both smiled.

Her friend moved on, and I asked Valerie what she did. She said she was a student at Seattle Pacific University and played basketball, but was considering transferring to another college.

It wasn't long before we started to talk about Jesus Christ. "I guess you could say I'm on a spiritual kick," Valerie said. "I'm hungry for God, and that's the most important thing in my life right now. I'm not looking for a man."

I liked her directness.

"That's cool," I answered. "I'm not looking for anyone either."

As we continued to talk, we sat down together on the sofa. We probably watched part of the game—at least she did. My attention was on her most of the time.

Valerie told me she came from a large family with one sister, four brothers, and two half-sisters from her dad's first marriage. That meant a family of eight children. I explained I also came from a similar background with two families because of my dad's first marriage.

After the game was over, I wanted to hang out with Valerie a little longer. I was just about to say, "I'm new to Seattle. Would you like to show me around the city?" when she stood up and walked over to Kendrick and Cindi. She said her goodbyes to them and headed toward the door.

I blew it there, I thought. *Oh, well—I guess I'll just head back to the hotel.* But then Valerie stopped and sat down at the other end of the couch where I now was.

"I thought you were leaving," I said, talking across the two or three people between us.

"Yeah, I was," she said.

"Where you going?"

"I don't know."

"Why don't you show me around Seattle?" I suggested. "I don't know anything about this town."

"Sure, that would be fun," she agreed. "I'll be your tour guide."

A few minutes later we left Kendrick's place, got into her little green Neon, and started our tour. First, we went downtown. It was the first time I had seen the Space Needle. From there we went to the Pike Place Market. She wanted me to see the fish market, where a customer selects a fish and the workers pick it up and throw it to the man behind the counter, who guts it for the purchaser. It was fun watching that.

◆ ❖ ◆

By the time we left Pike Place, the sun had started to set, and the evening had cooled off. After that, we mostly drove around and listened to music. To my amazement, we both liked to listen to the same artists: Stevie Wonder, Lenny Kravitz, and Donnell Jones.

What is this? I wondered. *This girl is really cool. This is sweet.* I also thought, *She's here and I'm here, and now I have somebody to hang around with.*

"Where do we go next?" I asked.

"I'd like to take you to where you'll play your games," she said.

I still didn't even know where the Seahawks played—and neither did Valerie. She took me to Safeco Field, which was the stadium where the Seattle Mariners baseball team played. Actually, the Seahawks stadium, the Kingdome, had just been blown up in order to build a new park, and our first games were to be played at Husky Stadium on the University of Washington campus. As little as I knew, I could still tell Valerie and I were definitely *not* at Husky Stadium. Still, I really didn't care where we went. I just wanted to be with her, and so I let things play out.

At Safeco Field, we looked it over from the outside.

"Hey, let's sneak in," I said.

"What?"

"Yeah, come on—let's sneak in."

Valerie hesitated a moment before she laughed and said, "Okay, let's do it."

We started to walk around the back where the loading docks were located so we could sneak in. Unbeknownst to us, that's where the security guard was stationed. We didn't see him till the last moment, because he wore a dark uniform and had his back to us. Then he turned around.

I decided to take the bold approach. "I'm Shaun Alexander," I said, "and I just got drafted to play here, and we wanted to come and see the stadium. They told me if I walked back here somebody would be able to show me around." Who "they" were I had no idea—those words just came out of my mouth.

The guard looked at me for a second. Then he said with a huge smile, "Well, Mr. Alexander, welcome to Seattle." He enthusiastically stretched out his hand and gave me a firm handshake. "Follow me."

The guard showed us the locker room first, then the field. There he explained how the retractable roof worked. We saw where the cameras were located, and he patiently answered every question.

I kept thinking, *This is sure the tightest first date I've ever been on.*

After our grand tour, we thanked the guard. As we walked toward the car, Valerie—who finally understood that this wasn't where I'd be playing—said, "I'm sorry, Shaun…you see, I have to confess something…I really don't know too much about football."

> **I'd met a lot of girls who acted pure and good at first, especially in public. Then as soon as we'd get alone, they'd change.** *Was she like the others?* **I wondered. I hoped not.**

"Oh, really?" I replied.

"But I'd like to learn," she continued. "My family is big into basketball and track, so I just thought you played here." So that was why she had taken me to the Mariners' stadium.

We laughed quite a bit over that. As we prepared to leave, she said, "Now I'm going to take you to the best sight in Seattle."

A few minutes later, she drove up a steep hill to the entrance of Gas Works Park. As we drove in, questions started to come into my mind about this woman I'd just met only hours ago. I'd met a lot of girls who acted pure and good at first, especially in public. Then as soon as we'd get alone, they'd change. *Was she like the others?* I wondered. I hoped not.

Valerie drove into the beautiful park as darkness had begun to take over. I'd figured it out now—she *was* like the others. *How am I going to get away from this girl?* I asked myself. *If I stay with her, how far do I go? How far is too far?*

I didn't want to get into this kind of head talk again. I didn't want to get into any kind of situation where I'd have to ask myself how far I should go. I felt I was past that kind of thing.

When we reached the parking lot, she said, "We've got to get out here and walk under that tree." She pointed. "There's a platform where we can stand and see all of downtown. That's the best sight in all of Seattle."

As we started over, I noticed two cars already parked with couples inside. *Okay, we're at the local make-out mountain,* I laughed to myself as we walked up to the site.

"All right, cover your eyes," she said, and she took my hand to lead me to the platform. Then, "Okay—open them."

I did—and the sight *was* beautiful. It had just turned dark, so all the blazing lights below made it a fantastic scene. I watched for several minutes. A cool wind began to blow. Valerie didn't have a coat, so I put my arm around her. Just as I did that, the question came into my mind—*What's going to happen now?*

"It's cold," she said, moving away. "Maybe we should go back to the car."

"Okay," I said, thinking how weird it was that we'd go sit in the car when those other couples were making out in their cars on both sides of us. *Is that what I want to do?* I asked myself.

As soon as we got inside the car, she started the engine and turned on the heater. The windows fogged up. She flipped on the radio and caught the middle of Stevie Wonder blasting away. I thought, *Oh yeah, Stevie—I mean, Oh no, Stevie.*

Then came something I'll never forget. Valerie dropped a CD, and both of us reached for it at the same time. We touched hands—and we both pulled away suddenly at the sensation. Then she started to laugh—I think both of us felt really awkward.

After we'd listened to the rest of the song, she said, "I really like Stevie Wonder."

"Yeah, me too," I said.

All the while, my thoughts continued to intrude. *What are you going to do, Shaun? Are you going to be an obedient man of God? Are you going to be a chump and take the easy way? Are you going to give in? What are you going to do?*

"Did you like the view?" Val asked.

"Yeah, it's tight," I said.

"I'm so glad you liked it," she said—and then, before I knew what was happening, she put the car in reverse and started to drive out of the park.

I felt confused. I almost asked, "What happened here?" Then I thought how funny it was—and I almost felt ashamed. I'd assumed she was going to make a move on me or had been waiting for me to make a move on her.

Instead, she had done exactly what she'd promised. She had taken me to the best sight in Seattle, we'd seen it—and now we were leaving.

This girl is something else, I thought admiringly.

As she pulled up to my hotel, Valerie asked, "What are you doing tomorrow?"

"I don't know," I replied. "I guess I'm not doing anything."

"My sister Kristin is a senior in high school," she said, "and she's got a track meet for the state championships tomorrow. I can pick you up if you want to go."

"Yeah—I'd like that," I said.

It was a date.

◆ ❖ ◆

The next morning Valerie came by at ten-thirty, and we left for the track meet. Her parents were going to be there, so I would have the chance to meet them.

"It's been a long time since I've been to a public event like this," I said as we arrived.

She seemed surprised, so I explained. "When I was at Alabama I had gotten such a big name I didn't go around in public just to hang out. Like this track meet. I was constantly getting mobbed for autographs and things like that."

"Is that so?" she remarked. "I don't understand people acting like that. Who's so good that people would mob them?"

"I don't know," I said, "but it was like that for me in Alabama."

A few minutes later, I sat down next to her mother and we started watching the track meet.

"I've never seen you before," Mrs. Boyd said. "Are you new in town?"

"Yes, ma'am," I said. I wasn't going to say anything more.

"That's good. So do you work here?"

"Yes, I do."

"You came here for a job?"

"Yeah, sure did."

"Mom!" Valerie broke in. "Shaun plays for the Seahawks."

"Oh, congratulations," she said. Then she turned away and kept watching the meet. She wasn't rude, but she was more interested in the meet than in talking to a celebrity—which I thought was cool. I didn't get that response too often. I didn't care for the celebrity business, and on that day, it was a relief to feel like I was with normal, friendly human beings.

Right about then, Valerie's father came back from the concession stand and sat down with us. After a race finished, he turned around to me and asked, "So you play with the Seahawks. What college did you go to?"

"Alabama," I said.

"Alabama? I know them," he said. "They win championships."

"Yes sir, we do." Mr. Boyd's response told me right then and there that he and I would get along just fine.

"Alabama—that's good, from what I've heard," Valerie's mom added. "I'm not too sure where the school is, though."

"It's in Tuscaloosa," I replied. "Have you ever heard of Bear Bryant?"

"Oh, of course. Bear Bryant," she said. "He was one of the best coaches of all time."

I agreed with her. "He passed a while ago, but Alabama is the school where he coached and won all those championships."

"You went to a very good school then," she said with a smile.

"I'm from Kentucky. Like most people in that area," I went on, "I pay attention to college basketball too."

"You know the Kentucky Wildcats?"

"Everyone in the state of Kentucky knows the Wildcats—at least everyone I know."

That started a good conversation about basketball. The Boyds were so down-to-earth, and the talk flowed easily. To them, I was just a boy Valerie had brought to a track meet, not a professional football player.

We had a great time while we finished watching the meet and were happy to see Kristin come in third in the hurdles. We walked down from the stadium to the parking lot, where we met her.

"Congratulations," I said to her, and shook her hand.

"Thank you," she said. She smiled, and I could easily see the family resemblance.

A few minutes later, I met Valerie and Kristin's youngest brother, Jason, who was a high school sophomore. He and his buddies stopped, and she introduced me to them.

As we were starting to leave, Jason's friends pulled him aside, and I heard one of them ask, "Do you know who your sister is with?"

I started to laugh, and I took Valerie's arm. "Come on, we've got to go."

"Shaun, I actually think they know who you are," she said as we walked away.

"Yeah—I think they do." I laughed again.

On the way back to my hotel, we stopped to eat, and she asked me, "What are you doing tomorrow?"

I thought, *I need to say whatever I said yesterday.* And I did.

"Well, I'm going to church tomorrow morning," she said. "I can pick you up if you want."

"Okay, that's cool," I said. "Tell me about your church."

She had grown up at Christian Faith Center in Seattle. The pastor there was Casey Treat. "You'll like Pastor Treat," she explained. "He's a real man of God, and the church is one of Seattle's biggest churches." The more she talked about it, the more eager I was to go.

The next morning Val picked me up. She was a little late so we couldn't find a parking spot nearby. As we started to walk toward the church we heard a man behind us call out, "Hey! Wait for me!"

There was no one else near us, so it was obvious he meant us. I turned to Valerie and asked, "Do you know that guy?"

She shook her head.

We kept on walking, but we slowed down so he could catch up to us before we reached the front door. The man didn't say another word but simply walked inside with us. Valerie led the way down the aisle. I followed, and the stranger came right behind me. She found a place for three, so we sat together.

I was amazed at the size of the building. I had grown up in a church of 150 members, and Calvary Baptist in Tuscaloosa had been large—but this building held thousands.

"Yes, it's a big church," Valerie said. "And you have to really get involved and become a part of it so that you warm into it."

Because we were so late, we missed most of the singing. Then Casey Treat stood up to preach. He was funny, but his words were powerful. At the end of his message, many people came to the altar to give their lives to Jesus Christ and to join the church.

As soon as the service was over, people started to walk out or pause to talk to each other. When I stood up, the man who had followed us into the building didn't move. I turned and glanced at Valerie, raising my eyebrows to ask, *What's with this?*

She shrugged.

I turned to him, thinking I could get him going, and said, "You've got a nice church."

"This isn't my church," he replied.

"Oh, you're from out of town like me," I said.

"No, no—I'm from here," he said. "I go to a different church."

"So why are you here today?" I asked.

"I felt...I just needed to..." His voice broke, and his eyes filled with tears. "My life is a mess." He told us he'd caught his wife cheating on him with his best friend. His wife had made him leave and wouldn't allow him to see their kids.

I stood and listened, but I didn't know what to say.

He went on. "No one in my family has ever been divorced before, so now I'm a disgrace to the rest of them. I don't know where to go or where to turn. I try to talk to my mom and dad, but they just look at me like I'm the one that's the problem."

Finally I said, "I pray to God I never have to go through what you're going through. But I know what your answer is." I told him how much Jesus loves him, and I quoted several Bible verses I thought would help him.

"I know all that," he said. Then he told me all the things he had tried to do to get his life in order.

I offered a couple more suggestions. He replied, "I've tried that too, but it didn't work."

Valerie had been listening but had said nothing the entire time. Finally, she moved right up to him and said, "That's your problem. You keep putting *I* in front of everything. You say, 'I'm doing this,' and 'I'm doing that.' Instead, you need to get on your knees and humble yourself." I was amazed at Val's boldness. She didn't scold—she just spoke in her natural, straightforward manner.

The man calmed down and nodded. "Yeah...you're right."

I knelt beside him and talked to him about what real commitment to Jesus means. This time he listened to every word without justifying his behavior. When I didn't know what else to add, I said, "Man, let's just pray."

I'd prayed with people before in church and in other places. Usually when two guys pray, most girls stay in the background. Because I had my eyes closed and had taken the guy's hand, I didn't pay any attention to Valerie—but when I opened my eyes, she started to pray for him just as fervently as I had. She had an arm around his shoulder.

Her passion amazed me. *This woman knows how to pray,* I realized.

After we finished, the man thanked us. "You're right. My wife did wrong, but I've been wrong too."

We never did figure out why he called out to us and followed us into the church. Neither of us ever saw him again—but we knew God had wanted us there to pray for him. As we walked out of the building, Valerie said with a smile, "Now we know why we were late for church."

I returned her smile. And I was thinking, *Now I know why I was sent to Seattle.* I had been there only three days, but I knew.

I had met my wife.

Chapter 12

FIRST PROFESSIONAL SEASON, 2000/2001

In May of 2000 I went through my first Seahawks minicamp. After that, I visited the city twice to look for a house. Of course, both times I called Valerie, and she picked me up at the airport. Not only did she help me find a house, she even helped me pick out the furniture.

Before I moved for good, however, Durran and I and some of our friends from Florence had a special trip in mind—a visit to King's Island, an amusement park near Cincinnati that our family had visited almost every year when I was growing up.

Besides just wanting to hang out together one more time before I left, we were also eager to try a new roller-coaster ride called the Son of the Beast. It was supposed to be the longest, fastest wooden roller coaster in the world and the first with a loop.

Brian, Josh, Ray, Scott, Durran, and I rode every other ride in the park first. Finally it was time for the big one—the Son of the Beast. The line for it was super long, but it gave us a great chance to talk about our lives and about our futures as we waited.

At one point Ray asked, "Shaun, besides your football career, what do you do for fun—real fun—out there in Seattle?"

"Well, nothing—at least so far," I said. "I've just been chilling and looking for stuff for my house."

"No—Shaun, I know you," he said. "You don't just sit around. What are you doing for *real* fun? What's taking up your time?"

It was finally time to admit what I hadn't yet told even my brother. "Well, to tell you the truth," I said, "I've been spending most of my time with a girl I met."

"*What?*" Ray's mouth dropped open. "Who is she?"

"Her name is Valerie Boyd," I said, "and—guys, this is the one." And I told them all about her.

"That's crazy, man." Ray shook his head and laughed. "Shaun, don't you remember what your cousin Michael said to you not long ago—and what Vicki said?"

I had to admit I'd forgotten about it. But when he mentioned it, the memory rushed back.

> "You ain't perfect, but you're consistent. I need that in *my* life."…He looked right at me and said, "Man, I'm through with what this world has been offering me. I'm not going to give the world my good times anymore."

"Both of them told you she was just around the corner," Ray reminded me. "That's *her,* man."

I had figured out Valerie was the girl for me, but I had totally blocked out the words of my cousins. *God is sure good to me,* I thought.

Ray was quiet for a while, and then he spoke up again. "Shaun, do you realize everything you do turns out great? You're blessed by the Lord—and you're the happiest person I've ever been around."

I was trying to take that in and figure out where the conversation was going when he added, "And you're consistent. You ain't perfect, but you're consistent. I need that in *my* life."

After a little longer he looked right at me and said, "Man, I'm through with what this world has been offering me. I'm not going to give the world my good times anymore."

We went on talking for quite a while about the impact my experiences had had on him. I sensed that something was going on inside him and that it was genuine, but he never opened up any further.

Two days later I left for Seattle.

But that wasn't the end of Ray's story. He went back to the church where he had grown up and gave his life to Christ. The following week he was baptized and joined the church. He's never been the same since. When he told me he was through giving his life to the world, that's exactly what he meant—he simply wasn't going to give the world his life. We have two choices in life: giving ourselves up to the world and its values and amusements—or we can give ourselves to Christ and let Him guide us. And when Ray did that, God led him to work with the youth at his church.

Whenever I think of Ray, I remember that amazing transformation. He had tried to fill this life with all the wrong things. At one time in his life he drank himself into a coma and was rushed to the hospital, where he flatlined. But he was revived—God wasn't finished with him yet. During his years in "the world" Ray had a lot of girlfriends and many drinking buddies and a few drug-using friends. All these experiences left him empty, but he found fulfillment in Jesus Christ.

Ray now has one of the largest youth ministries in Florence. He's also happily married with two awesome kids. Once Ray gave his life to Jesus, God revealed His plan for Ray's life—and it's an awesome plan.

This isn't to say that everyone who turns to God ends up in some kind of church ministry, like Ray, but I do believe every Christian has some way he or she can serve. There are always things we can do for God. And the great thing is, He never disappoints us like the world does.

I'll always be grateful that I was around godly men during my high school and college days and that they influenced my life so much. And I was excited to think about who God would provide as my friends in my new home of Seattle.

The first one He brought my way was James Mitchell, the pastor to college students at Antioch Bible Church. During my rookie year with the Seahawks he was one of our chaplains.

After he had been first introduced to us, I walked up to him and stuck out my hand to introduce myself—but he already knew who I was.

We started to talk, and I soon discovered he was a good listener. After that, we had many serious times together. James became a father figure to me in my early days in Seattle. Whenever I struggled with difficult questions about life, he was the man I contacted.

One big issue he helped me work through was the anger I felt about my dad. Even though it had been 12 years since Dad had left Mom, I still was dealing with the hurt and rejection I felt when it happened. I had carried it silently all those years. Not many people knew about it—but I did.

Growing up, I never saw my dad except at sporting events. When we did talk, sports was the only thing he brought up with me—and that made me even more angry. *Doesn't he care about anything else in my life?* I wondered. Don't get me wrong—I loved him being at my sports events, but it also fired me, because I felt like I was more than just a sports event. I wanted to know that Dad realized that too. At my most charitable moments, I just decided sports was the best he could do and he simply didn't know how to talk on a personal, father-to-son level.

On top of that, Durran and my half-brothers insisted I was the special son, like the way Tony said Dad had "put me in my shoes." I never understood how they could say that or why they felt that way.

"You're like Joseph in the Old Testament," Durran explained. "You get treated special because you're the youngest son." He wasn't mad like some of my other brothers were, but those were the facts as he saw them. "Yes, Shaun—you're special to Dad."

Special? I had never felt special around my father—except on the football field.

After I talked all this over with James, he said, "You're bitter, aren't you, Shaun?"

I hadn't thought of that word before, but I realized he was right.

He explained to me the danger of bitterness—where it comes from and how it can destroy a person or kill relationships. I realized that my attitude affected many areas of my life—not just my relationship with my dad.

James helped me learn to let go of these hurt feelings. It wasn't easy, and it didn't happen in one week, but slowly I was able to change.

After James and I had talked about bitterness several times, I finally decided to call my father. I let him know how I felt and how hurt I had been when he'd talked to me about nothing but sports.

My words really shocked him. "A lot of times you're the only one I talked to," he responded, "because I've always felt like you're the one who's going to be there for me."

"Why? What are you talking about?" I asked.

Then Dad told me about the death of his father—my grandfather—and how it changed his attitude toward his sons. When my grandfather died, there was no one who wanted to step up and make arrangements for the funeral. My grandmother didn't want to do it, and neither did any of my grandfather's brothers and sisters. There was no one who cared enough to assume the responsibility. So Dad took the initiative and arranged for the funeral and burial plot for his father.

Then Dad told me about the summer my grandmother died and he'd taken me to her funeral. At the time, Donte worked in Orlando, Florida, so he couldn't go to the service. Ronnie and Tony were both in the military, so they weren't able to attend. Durran was at a special event at for school involving the Governor's Scholar Program, so he couldn't attend either. That meant I was the only one of Dad's five sons who could be with him at his mother's funeral.

I didn't have much choice about whether to go. I knew Grandma had died, and that was about all. Because I was young and didn't really know her, I didn't think much about it. I remembered almost nothing about that day.

But Dad remembered.

While we sat at the funeral, Dad cried a lot. I was sitting next to him, and people would come by and ask him who I was. He would tell them, "This is my youngest son, Shaun."

At that time I had no way of knowing what was going on inside his mind or how the deaths of his parents had affected him. But now, as we talked on the phone, Dad told me that after the funeral he had promised himself something. Although his relationships with his other sons weren't that great, from that day on, he vowed, he would be around for *this* son—his son Shaun. He told me he didn't want to turn out like his dad…with no one to be there for him when he needed someone.

Because he never said anything to me about that decision, I didn't know why things changed in our relationship. From sixth to eighth grade, Dad had never shown any interest in my games—and then all of a sudden, in tenth grade, after my grandmother's funeral, he started coming to every football game.

At first I thought, *Dad doesn't turn up at any of my games for years, and now when I'm a Little League all-star about to play high school ball, all of a sudden he wants to show up. Forget it!* I was angry.

Though Dad continued to come to my games, he never explained why. I was still angry, but I kept the anger stuffed inside.

But that day when I was talking to him on the phone about everything, he made it clear. He said, "I told myself, *I'm glad I can grab one of my sons instead of losing all of them.*"

Later, as I pondered that talk with my dad, I wrote in my journal,

> Maybe he doesn't know how to love his son because his father didn't
> know how to love him…Never judge a person because of how
> they treat you until you learn what they are going through.

Perhaps Dad was doing what he thought true love was. Showing up at sporting events was the only way he knew how to express love to me. Once I acknowledged that, I was able to push away my resentment.

I've learned not to judge others. I never know the full story of why people act the way they do. It only hurts me when I allow their actions to cause resentment in me. But if I can forgive and move on, I don't have to deal with all that anger and bitterness that can ultimately destroy me.

Life's too short. It's just not worth it.

I went through my rookie year with the Seahawks without playing much. Ricky Watters was the running back, and he was very good. I watched him and learned from the way he played. Ricky had one more year on his contract, so I assumed I wouldn't play much my second season either.

Naturally, I would have liked it if they had said, "Shaun, you're going to be our running back." But professional football seldom works that way, and I knew it going in.

While I was waiting for my chance to play, I took advantage of speaking opportunities that came my way. I was determined I was going to use the platform God was giving me. I decided I could travel around the country and talk to people about my faith in Jesus Christ as the opportunities opened up. I saw I could build up the Shaun Alexander Foundation and help more needy kids. And that's what I did.

I was now a professional football player.

I was living a great life that God had made possible.

Is it any wonder I daily repeated aloud my life verse, Psalm 37:4—"Delight yourself in the Lord and he will give you the desires of your heart"?

Chapter 13

SECOND SEASON, 2001/2002

After the end of my first season with the Seahawks, I agreed to go to another FCA camp in June—this one in Bristol, Tennessee. By now I was excited whenever I was able to go to a camp. I had seen how effective they were in reaching kids, and it pumped me up to be a part of what God was doing and to know I could be influential in the lives of some of these kids.

Though the camps ask the staff to get there on Saturday, two days early, this time a special event kept me from doing that. I had already made plans to fly to Omaha to attend the wedding of my former roommate, Reggie Grimes, to his college sweetheart, Mikaela. So it wasn't until Sunday that I flew to Bristol to get ready for the camp, which was yet another great experience for me.

◆ ❖ ◆

After the camp, I continued to speak during the months of June and July. For example, on June 27, I spoke at a youth rally in Birmingham. The next day I spoke at a football camp conducted by Sam Shade, a former defensive back for Alabama and the Cincinnati Bengals. On July 7, I flew to North Carolina to do FCA's Black Mountain Two.

While there, I glanced at the calendar one day and counted: I had only 16 days remaining before training for my second season as a Seahawk was to begin. I had been so busy speaking, I had neglected one very important activity for a professional athlete—I had hardly worked out the entire summer.

Reality set in. I was in North Carolina, and I wasn't in good shape. I tried to calm myself down by remembering, *Hey, I'm just a backup for Ricky Watters. It's only my second year and Ricky is the man.*

During a break at camp, I decided to walk down the side of the mountain. I broke into a run, and about halfway down, I stepped wrong and twisted my ankle. It was sore enough that I couldn't run any further.

"God, help me!" I cried out in desperation. "I need to get into shape. What I am going to do?"

I didn't hear a voice, but I felt an inner assurance—as if God had said, *Didn't I tell you to go out and speak? I'll give you what you need for the season.*

I felt an immediate sense of peace. I also reminded myself again that Ricky Watters was still there. Everything would be all right.

As I sat at the side of the road, I felt God speaking to me again. *You've trusted Me in the past. Why are you now trying to figure it out without Me?*

I limped back up the hill, embarrassed at hobbling along, yet laughing most of the way and telling God, "All right, then. I trust You."

The 2001 football season was ready to start. I had gone through training camp as usual. The night before our first game, I went to a Bible study with Pastor Ken "Hutch" Hutcherson from Antioch Bible Church in Seattle. It was an intense and enlightening study for me, especially when Pastor Hutch emphasized the need to depend totally on the Lord. I was reminded of what God had said to me at the camp only weeks before. Depending on Him was exactly what I needed to do. So as I listened, I promised myself I would depend more fully on His strength and guidance.

Our first game was against the Cleveland Browns. Ricky had a good game. We won 9–6. Our team was off to a good start, and all of us were pumped.

Early Tuesday morning, two days after the Cleveland game, my cell phone rang. The screen showed it was from my friend Jason List, whom I still call my little brother. I wondered why he was calling so early. Then my house phone began to ring—my caller ID showed it was Durran. Several other calls were trying to come in on my voice mail.

Jason called again, and I answered.

"What's going on?" I asked.

He just said, "Shaun, turn on your TV."

I ran to the TV. It was Tuesday, September 11, 2001. They were showing the video of a plane that had just crashed into one of the Twin Towers of the World Trade Center.

Like other Americans, I was horrified. "What in the world is happening?" I said aloud—and just as I finished that sentence, the second plane hit the Towers. I didn't know what to think or how to respond. I had friends who worked in New York. All I could do was wonder if they were safe. That tragedy was as emotionally difficult for me as it was for nearly all of us. Football—and practice—was cancelled for the rest of the week while America mourned.

◆ ❖ ◆

Our next game was against Philadelphia, and they beat us. Then on September 30, we played the Oakland Raiders. Near the end of the game, Ricky was running with the ball, and a Raiders player hit him hard.

He didn't get up.

As we all watched, they carried him off the field. We knew he wouldn't be able to go back in.

I said to myself, *Here it goes again.* Jason Colemire had gone down in high school and that had brought me into the game. At Alabama, Dennis Riddle had gone down, and that had made the way for me. Now it was Ricky. Of course I wanted to play, but I hated to get thrown into the game because someone else had been injured.

After I was in, I ran for a touchdown—but it was too late. The Raiders beat us 38–14. Even worse, none of us on the team knew how seriously Ricky was hurt.

It turned out his shoulder was broken—which meant I would be starting for at least several more games.

Next, we faced the Jacksonville Jaguars. I played against Fernando Bryant, their starting cornerback, who had been a close friend in my days at Alabama. We played a good game, and I scored two touchdowns with 170 yards rushing. I could feel myself getting into the groove, and I said to myself, *Here we go—this is it—and I'm kicking it back up again.* It felt great!

After that, we played the Denver Broncos. During the first play of the game, I gained six yards; on the second, three; on the third, four more—and we had a first down. On the fourth play, I ran for a 60-yard touchdown. Everybody was going crazy, with shouts, yells, and whistles. I couldn't get the grin off my face.

I was jazzed. *We're doing it now! We're doing it now! We're taking off!* I was starting to step into that zone—I knew now I really was going to be a good pro player.

Silently I praised God. Even though I hadn't worked out during the off-season, God was still in control. Not only that, but His promise that He would take care of me if I depended totally on Him was proven true again.

On November 11, 2001, we were going to play the Raiders again. I'd started every game since Ricky had been injured. My stats were good, but we were a 3-4 ball club at that point. We needed more wins.

I don't know why, but on Saturday night—the night before the game against the Raiders—I had a feeling that the game would be a monster: a big win for us. ESPN was going to telecast it Sunday night, so I called Mom and told her, "Make sure you watch this game—it's going to be exciting."

I also called Durran, and then the Sellers in Tuscaloosa. I left a message on their answering machine: "Make sure you watch the game Sunday night. I'm going off." By that I meant I was going to do something outstanding.

Maybe that sounds like bragging—I didn't mean it that way. I just knew I was going to be in a zone again.

I went to bed that night like normal—but sleep didn't come. As I lay there, for some reason I kept thinking about Jason List's younger brother, Michael. Earlier I had taken Michael to one of the Black Mountain camps. At FCA camps, kids learn the truth about living their faith in the world. Most of them listen and try to put the teachings into practice. We teach them about the great challenges before them and push them to make a decision for or against following God. If they declare their decision to obey Him, they have to step up and start living their faith.

I don't know why, but I couldn't get Michael off my mind. Finally, I got out of bed and started to write him a letter. I wrote about life and the decisions we make, and I emphasized the importance of closeness to the Lord.

I wanted to make sure Michael stayed with the faith. I became so involved in writing that letter, I couldn't put it aside. I felt a deep emotional involvement, and several times I had to wipe away the tears. I cared very much for Michael—I didn't want him to go astray.

Finally finished, I rolled into bed and slept for maybe four hours before I had to be at a breakfast and then go on to some team meetings. With so little sleep, I should have been wiped out physically and emotionally, but I wasn't. In fact, I felt rested and alert.

> I knew then—in a way I hadn't realized before—that not only was I really in the NFL and was going to be around for a while, but also that I had the potential to do things with our team that hadn't been done before.

I felt on top all day. And when it came time to play the Raiders that night, I broke several runs and made my longest carry since turning professional—an 88-yard touchdown run. It was an amazing game, and I finished with 266 yards and three touchdowns.

Someone told me it was the fourth-best game in NFL history. I didn't check that, but I knew it was definitely the best game in Seahawks history. Even more meaningful to me, it was Shaun Alexander's best game to date.

Afterward, several teammates came up to me, and one of them said, "You *knew*, didn't you?"

"Yeah," I said. "I had a feeling."

"I felt it too," he answered.

At the time, the Raiders had one of the best defenses in the NFL, which made our victory even more exciting. I knew then—in a way I hadn't realized before—that not only was I really in the NFL and was going to be around for a while, but also that I had the potential to do things with our team that hadn't been done before.

I had had a couple of good games previously that season. But after that game, remembering how I had stayed up late in obedience to God to write that letter to Michael, I felt God showing me something. Because I had made Him my first priority, He was smiling on me as if to say, *I'm with you, Shaun. I'll bless your playing.*

I continued to play in our next several games. We beat Buffalo, lost to Kansas City, and won again in San Diego. By December, Ricky's shoulder was well enough for him to return to the field. That was hard—but Ricky was my friend, and he had cheered me on. Now he was ready to play again, and as much as I wanted to be out on the field, it was his position, and my role was to stay on the bench and cheer *him* on. I was then—and still am—a big Ricky Watters fan.

I did want to play, though—which was natural. I kept thinking, *Here are two guys—Ricky and me—who love each other, and we both want to play the same position. How is that going to work?*

Just before we played the Denver Broncos we had a big meeting and talked about what to do for the game. Coach Holmgren and Ricky decided they were going to start me, and then Ricky would run certain packages during the game.

That plan *sounded* great—however, it didn't work great.

Neither Ricky nor I were into the rhythm. I was used to getting the ball, but in that game I couldn't get into it. Ricky was used to being on the field and controlling the flow of the game. Now he was coming in off the bench. We both played, but there was no magic for either of us. They beat us 20–7.

The next week, on December 16, we played against the Dallas Cowboys. Five of my college buddies came into town to see the game. I was relaxed and laid back. "I'm glad you came, and I hope you'll enjoy the game," I said, "but I probably won't play a lot."

Ricky was back, and he was *the* running back. I knew he would start the game, and I was all right with that. "My time will come," I told my buddies. "I'd much rather have us win than for my stats to be built up."

When the game started, Ricky went out strong. He was having a good game, and I sat on the bench and cheered him on.

Then all of a sudden, play was stopped. Ricky was under the pile. It turned out he was hurt again. This time it was a broken collarbone, so he was out of the game.

I could hardly believe it. I wanted to play, but I hated that Ricky had gotten hurt. I went into the game and scored a touchdown. From then on, I was in the groove and played my best. We won 29–3.

The following week, we flew to New York, and on Sunday, December 23, we played against the Giants. As the fourth quarter was near its end—with a minute and 40 seconds left in the game, and no time-outs—we were four points ahead. We had punted the ball to their 8-yard line—and they drove 92 yards, beating us 27–24.

That was terrible—a really bad ending to one of the best weeks of my life. (I'll explain more later as to why it was such a great week.)

Our next game was against San Diego. We won, ending up that season with 9 wins and 7 losses—a winning season. And it turned out to be a good season for me personally. I ended up with 1318 yards rushing and 16 touchdowns.

At the end of the season, Ricky retired. He was very gracious and wished me well. "All right, Shaun," he told me. "You're ready to become the man."

He knew, and so did I: My career was about to take off.

It was my time.

Chapter 14

OPTIMUS PRIME

Though I knew the third day after I met Valerie that she was the woman God had chosen for me, she didn't know that yet. For a while, she was still on the kick of our just being "good friends."

She later told me that one special date changed her mind. It was on the Fourth of July, 2000. We had driven to Gas Works Park in Seattle again, and while we were there, Valerie prayed silently, *God, I have feelings for Shaun as a friend. We enjoy hanging out together. But if I'm supposed to have any stronger, more serious feelings, You've got to put them in me.*

Because it was a holiday, the park was extremely crowded. In the press of people, I took her hand and pulled her close so we could maneuver through the crowd.

That was such a simple act. But she later told me, "That was the moment I knew I loved you." Though I hadn't done anything unusual, something about my touch had awakened her feelings for me. God had quickly answered her prayer. However, at that time neither of us was ready to say anything about our feelings.

By August, Val and I had been friends for two months. After having been to the Seahawks training camp preparing for a preseason game, I came home on a Tuesday.

That night something happened to me—something many people will think is totally bizarre—but it's true. I had a dream that night, and for the following two nights as well. In the dream that first night, I was sitting on the leather couch in my TV room. Valerie walked in and slid down over the arm of the couch next to me.

"Hey," she said.

We looked at each other. Then I pulled her close, and we started to kiss. Soon we went into the bedroom and had sex. When we were finished, I got up and walked over to the mirror, angry at myself. In the dream I stared at myself, thinking, *I'm a Christian. What am I doing? How could I let this happen?*

After I awoke that morning, I tried to go about my day normally, just telling myself that every guy dreams about girls and sex now and then. It's not really a big deal. Even though I said those things to myself, I couldn't forget how real the dream had been, and worse, how guilty I had felt.

That night I dreamed again. I was on the couch when Valerie came into the TV room. She slid over the arm of the couch next to me.

I stared at her and asked myself, *Is this going to happen again?*

Just like the night before, we ended up in the bedroom. And afterward I looked into the mirror, angry at myself again. As I stared at my reflection, I heard the words, *If you hadn't kissed her, it never would have happened.*

Okay, I decided. *I get the message.*

But on the third night, I had the dream one more time. This time, however, I vowed to myself, *I'm not going to kiss her.* But as we sat next to each other in the TV room, that resolve lasted only a few minutes. Then I grabbed her, and we started to kiss. We ended up in the bedroom. Afterward, I got up and stared at myself in the mirror again.

In the dream, I heard the same voice as I had the night before: *If you hadn't kissed her, it would never have happened.*

That day was Friday. I thought about the dream a few times later on, but not a lot because my family was in town and I was busy with them.

That night I didn't have the dream again.

On Sunday after the church service, I was heading to my house. Valerie called to me from her car and asked, "Shaun, are you going back to your house?"

"Yes," I said. "Why?"

"I've got something I really need to talk to you about."

We agreed that she'd drop by later—and she did.

When she walked in, I was sitting on the black leather couch in my TV room. I hadn't even been thinking about the dreams. Then she slid down the arm of the couch—and the three dreams flooded back into my mind. I was totally shaken. *It's happening. The dream is coming true. Now what?*

Valerie gazed at me for several seconds before she said, "Shaun, I know we're just friends. We've only known each other two months, and we're not even seriously girlfriend and boyfriend or anything like that. But I've got to tell you something. If anything ever comes about between us—like if we all of a sudden start dating and it becomes serious—well, I've prayed about it, and…"

I nodded, trying to figure out what she was trying to say.

She took a deep breath and gazed right at me. "Shaun, God told me we shouldn't kiss each other until we're married."

My mouth dropped open. I was unable to say anything for a second. Then I shook my head. "Valerie, you won't believe this, but…" And then I told her about the three nights of dreams.

I could hear the relief in her voice. "So you don't think I'm weird?" she asked.

The understanding we reached that night became the basis of our dating life. We held hands, and when she left, we hugged goodbye, but we did nothing beyond that. Both of us knew what God wanted. Most of all, I wanted to be obedient.

I know this part of our life together sounds crazy, and my non-Christian friends (and even some Christians) thought I was strange. I want to make it clear, however, that as weird as it may have sounded, neither of us ever felt we had to defend our decision. We knew what God had told us to do. That was enough.

We had our temptations—more than once. We finally decided to set up some boundaries to help us. For example, Valerie said, "Shaun, I can't be at your place after it gets dark." Sometimes she'd come to my house to eat after a game, but we decided she would leave immediately afterward. We couldn't sit and watch a movie together because we knew we were becoming serious about how we felt toward each other. We both knew it wouldn't have taken much for us to act as if we were married.

This may sound like a downer, but I can tell you that I saw Valerie for who she really is—a virtuous woman of God. As a result, my love for her increased steadily.

There was only one time when I doubted what should happen. After Valerie and I had known each other about a year, one of my spiritual mentors from Houston, Ramon Diaz, and his wife, Suzanne, went to dinner with me. As we ate, I told them about how special Valerie was. But even as I spoke, I was preparing to dump her. Don't ask—I can't explain the reason, and I don't even try.

But later that evening Suzanne said, "Shaun, I had a dream the other night, and in this dream you were running away from the church and from Valerie."

"What's that all about?" I asked.

"I don't know," she replied. "I just saw you running away in my dream. I'm telling you this because I think you need to pray seriously about your decisions, especially in the near future."

No one knew about either my deep feelings for Valerie or what I was getting ready to do. I knew I faced a spiritual test. I liked Valerie and she liked me, but I didn't know what was supposed to happen. As Ramon, Suzanne, and I went on talking, I was silently telling God, *Thanks, Lord, for letting me hear this admonition—I'm going to obey Your plan.* Being obedient was all I knew to do. As in the past, it was a matter of trusting God to lead me in all I do.

Over the next couple of weeks, I prayed more. Valerie and I talked often and became even closer than we had been. We were able to talk about our family issues and some deep problems neither of us had ever told anyone else. As we opened ourselves up to each other and talked about our insecurities and weaknesses, I felt my feelings for her growing deeper each day.

That unusual dinner with Ramon and Suzanne happened in the spring of 2001, and by winter I was ready to ask Val to marry me. As I mentioned in the last chapter, we had a game with the Giants on Sunday, December 23.

My upcoming trip to New York City reminded Valerie of her friend who lived there, and she mentioned she wanted to visit her.

"I think you ought to do that," I said. "If you do it when I'm in New York, you can also come to the game."

Valerie decided it was a great idea.

I started to cook up my plans.

Val flew to New York on Wednesday. The next evening I drove to her parents' home, which was in Olalla, Washington. In the middle of eating supper, I laid down my fork and asked the Boyds, "Do you all know why I'm here?"

"Of course," Momma Boyd said. "You wanted a good home-cooked meal."

"No, that's not the reason," I said with a laugh. "Valerie is in New York City. When I get there for the game, I want to ask her to marry me. But first, I want your permission."

Well, they both were ecstatic. I don't even remember how they actually said yes, but I got the idea they had no objections.

◆ ❖ ◆

Our team flew into New York Friday night. After practice Saturday morning, I called a friend, "Joe the Cop" as we called him, to take Valerie and me around to see the sights. I had already bought a beautiful ring with diamonds and hearts across the band, and I had heard of a famous restaurant in New York called the Tavern on the Green. I decided that's where I'd propose.

Joe picked Valerie up before he drove to our team hotel to pick me up. We had until eight that evening, which was when I had to be back. We went shopping and saw many of

> I looked at my watch. It was 7:20. I had to get back to the hotel by 8:00 and needed 30 minutes to get there. *I still haven't given her the ring, I thought... What am I going to do?*

the famous places in Manhattan, such as Rockefeller Center. Twice, Valerie accidentally bumped me, and I was afraid she'd figure out what I was carrying in my pocket.

When we started dating, Valerie had jokingly asked, "So when do you want to get married?"

"It will be sooner rather than later." That was always my evasive answer.

To her credit, she'd never pushed.

As we ate at the Tavern on the Green that evening, I kept thinking, *I need to find exactly the right moment to ask her.* Food seemed to be coming at us every few minutes, so I couldn't do it then. I wanted it to be a special moment when we were alone.

When we finished, I looked at my watch. It was 7:20. I had to get back to the hotel by 8:00 and needed 30 minutes to get there. *I still haven't given her the ring yet,* I thought. I felt sick inside. *What am I going to do?*

As we left the restaurant, Joe was standing outside. He smiled and announced, "Mr. Alexander, your horse and carriage await."

I silently thanked God. I knew Valerie would say yes to my proposal, but I wanted to make it a special, perfect memory for her.

We stepped inside the carriage and rode through Central Park. After maybe five minutes I called out to the driver, "Stop the horse for a minute."

As soon as he'd stopped, I turned to Valerie. "Do you remember when I told you I wanted to get married sooner rather than later?"

"Of course I remember," she replied.

I pulled out the ring.

Her eyes widened…she smiled at me. "It's sooner," I said. "Valerie—will you marry me?" Surprised and delighted, she said yes!

After taking us through the rest of Central Park, the driver brought us back to the Tavern on the Green. Joe was waiting. It was 7:45. We hurried into his car and raced back to the hotel. Before the car even came to a stop,

I jumped out and ran into the meeting room, arriving just in the nick of time.

The pregame meeting went well. Afterward, I went to my room and called Val. We talked for a bit, and after that I called my family and everybody else I could think of. Everyone was hugely excited. Needless to say, so was I.

Finally, I knew I had to sleep. Just as I turned off the lights, I said, "All right, God—I need to have one special game tomorrow because everyone is going to wonder if this has distracted me. Please, God, don't let that happen. Help me play well."

God answered that prayer. I felt fine the next day and was able to concentrate. I ended up with two touchdowns, one rushing and one receiving, and I rushed for more than 100 yards. We were winning the game and had punted them down to the eight yard line with a minute and 40 seconds left in the game, as I described earlier, but they drove the length of the field and beat us.

Still, even if we lost the game, I had won Valerie.

Valerie and I were married five months later, on May 18, 2002, at Florence Baptist Church in Florence, Kentucky. Because I had so much family there, it was easier to fly in 30 people from Val's family than to try to do everything in Seattle.

Some of our friends still talk about our wedding. Our pastor, Casey Treat, performed the ceremony, and everything was just right. Seven hundred people attended our reception. I had so many family members there that I was constantly saying to Val, "This is my cousin..." or "This is my uncle..." And the music was outstanding. Some of my friends who were singers performed, and they were a big hit.

One of my other friends who was there commented, "This is a celebration, not a wedding."

I liked that.

We honeymooned on St. John Island in the Virgin Islands for two weeks.

◆ ❖ ◆

When I tell the story about Val and me, people usually ask, "After you were engaged, did you kiss her?"

No, I didn't—just as she and I had resolved. The first time I kissed her was at the altar after Pastor Treat said, "You may now kiss your bride."

It was worth the wait.

◆ ❖ ◆

Later that year, I spoke to a high school student body at John Croyle's Big Oak Ranch in Alabama. My talk was about purity and love and relationships. As I spoke about those things, I was reminded of a story.

At Christmastime, Mom used to tell us to write down everything we wanted. Durran and I used to compete—if he wrote 10 items, I'd write 11; if he wanted 14, I'd have 16. By the time we finished our lists, we both had about 40 things we wanted. We knew Mom couldn't afford all those toys and clothes. She'd always tell us, "Now you boys go back and put a star by the gift you want the most."

There's only one time I can recall what I put a star beside. The big toy in those days was Transformers. The leader of the good guys was called Optimus Prime—a red loading truck that transforms into a robot.

When Christmas morning came that year, before we headed off for the celebration at my grandparents' house, the three of us sat in the front room of our apartment and opened our presents. As expected, Mom gave us T-shirts, underwear, socks, and jeans. All the usual stuff.

But after that, we opened the toys. We received G.I. Joes and several He-Man characters and eagerly started to play with them.

Then it hit me. I had put a star by Optimus Prime. So I said, "Hey, Mom—we've opened up all our gifts, and I didn't get Optimus Prime."

"Oh, that's right!" she said. "Let me get it." So she went to the coat closet where she always hid the good gifts and pulled it out. It wasn't wrapped—she must have forgotten she had put it there.

I opened it up and transformed it about five million times. I loved it. And a thought hit me. I wondered what would have happened if I hadn't asked Mom for the Optimus Prime. Now I know my mother loves us, but she's one of those people who, if we have what we want right then, will give the other presents to somebody who doesn't have any gifts. That's probably where I get this desire to give. I want to help other people and be involved in blessing their lives.

I told the students at Big Oak Ranch that story and said, "This has to do with relationships. And it helps me understand a little more about God. We all want to marry somebody special. There was one girl I looked at as if she were one of those He-Man toys we received. I enjoyed hanging out with her, but the relationship wasn't Optimus Prime. Everybody needs to understand that God wants to give us what we most desire but won't give it to us until we're ready to put away all the other toys. God wants to give us what we desire—but we must truly desire it." I wrapped up by saying, "Valerie is my Optimus Prime."

God's best is always worth the wait.

After I finished speaking, John Croyle said, "Optimus Prime? *Optimus* is like the top choice—the optimum choice—and *prime* is the highest quality. So Shaun, you got the number-one choice—the number-one quality."

Everyone applauded.

Many times I gaze at my wife and think, *Yes, Valerie is my Optimus Prime.*

Chapter 15

THREE SIGNIFICANT
NFL GAMES

As I went through my third season with the Seahawks and entered the fourth season, it was pretty easy to point to my three best NFL games so far.

The first would have to be the Raiders game on November 11, 2001, which I mentioned earlier. It was one of those games where I stepped into a zone. In those moments, I felt—and still feel, when it happens—as if I'm moving in a different world. I was carrying the ball and just knew that nothing could stop me. It was the first time that had happened since I had entered the NFL.

◆ ❖ ◆

The second of those three best games took place during my third year in the NFL, the 2002/2003 season.

That was a tough year. I had expected the Seahawks to go in there and be good. We had come off a season with nine wins and seven losses. I'd finally had a whole summer of training as the starting tailback.

And Trent Dilfer was our quarterback. During my rookie year, he'd won the Super Bowl as a member of the Baltimore Ravens. He was going to be our starting quarterback, and I thought for sure it was going to be our year.

I was mistaken. We had problems.

Trent tore his knee. Offensive tackle Walter Jones held out on signing his contract. Floyd "Pork Chop" Womack, our other key offensive tackle, twisted an ankle. All that was rough on the team's chemistry, and as a result, I had to play with a number of newer players.

We played the first game of the season against the Raiders in Oakland, and it went as it usually does in Oakland—they whipped us. They knocked out both our first- and second-string quarterbacks, and they beat us up bad.

I had 36 yards rushing in that game and one touchdown. We were embarrassed. We went from there to play the next game at home against Arizona. I did get better—by one whole yard—with 37 yards rushing. During one of my runs in that game, I spun around and somebody put his hands on my face mask and scratched the cornea of one of my eyes. I had to wear a visor for the rest of the year.

That's the way the season went—we had one problem after another. We played our third game against the Giants in New York. At the beginning of the game I thought, *This is my town—the place where I proposed to Valerie. We're going to do it.*

Again, I was wrong.

They beat us soundly. It was probably the most boring game the fans ever watched. The score was 9–6, with five field goals and no touchdowns. Again, I had only 37 yards rushing.

People began to talk negatively about me, saying things like, "Shaun was only good for one year." "Maybe last year was a fluke for him." And the worst comment of all: "Since Shaun got married, he's not playing as well now." I never could figure out how getting married might have affected my playing.

Nevertheless, our team started off 0 and 3, and I began to ask myself: *Shaun, did you train hard? Did you prepare for this season?*

Yes, I answered myself. *I worked faithfully with the sprint coaches and lifting coaches. I cut down on my traveling and speaking engagements. This has been, in fact, the hardest I've ever worked.*

◆ ❖ ◆

Just before the game against the Minnesota Vikings—which is my second choice for a memorable game—I was sitting in the locker room next to Heath Evans, our backup fullback. Heath had graduated from Auburn, our rival in college. As Seahawks, we'd become good friends. By that time, we'd already been playing together for a year.

I told Heath, "I'm really nervous about this game." He asked me why.

"I don't know," I said. "But nervousness for me is a good thing. There's something going on inside me. When I get nervous I can't think about fixing it. I only can think about letting God take over."

"Then don't worry about it," Heath said and slapped me on the back. "You're going to have an awesome game."

The first drive of the game, we pushed hard and finally moved the ball down to the goal line. I took the ball, dove over someone, and we had a touchdown.

We were up 7–0.

We got the ball again and were driving hard. It was third down—Trent, our quarterback, had called the play—but the center snapped the ball early, so everybody was startled. Trent just turned around and handed me the ball, so I ran, broke a tackle, and scored. I had two touchdowns in the first quarter.

We were on top and doing well.

The second quarter started, and a screen pass was called. I caught the ball, turned inside, and cut back outside. At that moment I realized I had outrun everybody. It became an 80-yard touchdown reception.

When we kicked off, Tim Terry, one of our men on the kickoff team, hit a Viking hard, forcing a fumble that we recovered.

Three plays later, I was handed the ball again, and I raced for my fourth touchdown.

We kicked off to the Vikings again—and as before Tim Terry hit their ball carrier, knocking him out of the way. That second hit was harder. The Vikings fumbled the ball, and we jumped on it yet again. When they gave me the ball, I took off and scored once more.

I had five touchdowns in the first half. We ended up winning 48–23.

◆ ❖ ◆

After the game, I thought about the weeks before, when I was being ridiculed and people had asked, "Is it your offensive line, Shaun?" "Is it your coach?" "Is it *you?*"

I had always answered, "No, it's *football*. It's all part of the game." I didn't want to blame anybody. When times are tough, we have to keep on going. Nothing is gained by playing the blame game.

And I became the first person—and still the only one in NFL history—to score five touchdowns in one half. It was an amazing game.

◆ ❖ ◆

> **The doctor reached me on my cell phone.**
> **"Are you at the hospital yet?"**
> **"Oh, no—not yet," I said calmly. "I'm at the house, and Valerie has already left..."**
> **"You need to get there. *Fast.*"**

The third-best game came early in my fourth season, a home game for us against the St. Louis Rams. By then Valerie and I were expecting a baby, and it was almost due.

The morning of September 21, which was game day, I stayed at a hotel in Seattle with the other team members. I woke up about eight and went down to eat breakfast with the guys. After I came back to my room, Valerie called on my cell phone.

"I think today is the day," she said. "I probably need to go to the hospital."

"Really?" I asked. "Are you sure?"

"Well, the contractions have started," she said.

That was all I needed to hear. Heath Evans drove me to our house to get my car so I could drive to the hospital. I think Heath was more nervous than either of us. Valerie and I are both pretty laid back. We take life as it comes.

While I was still at home, the doctor reached me on my cell phone. "Are you at the hospital yet?" he asked.

"Oh, no—not yet," I said calmly. "I'm at the house, and Valerie has already left for the hospital with her mother."

"You need to get there," he said. *"Fast."*

As it turned out, I arrived before he did. When he got there, he explained what would happen during the birthing process. Both Valerie and I were confident it was going to be a good birth with no complications.

Valerie is such a soldier. In the hospital room, she put on a CD and calmly listened to the group Third Day. After she dilated to ten centimeters, she started to push, as the doctor had instructed her. Between contractions she relaxed and listened to the music again. Her mom and my mom were both there, and so were Val's best friend, Dominique; Heath's wife, Beth Ann; and Val's sister Kristin.

At 12:37 PM we had a healthy baby daughter, who we named Heaven Nashay. We found *Nashay* in a biblical-meaning book, and it means *God's glory* or *God's purpose.*

Right after the nurse gave Heaven to me, I held her up and felt just like the Lion King when he held his son high for everyone to see. I wanted to lift her up to the sky.

Then I cut the umbilical cord and put Heaven on Valerie's chest. We cleaned her and asked everyone to leave the room for a little while. When we were alone, Val and I prayed for Heaven and for her future, vowing, "God, whatever you want us to do with this child, we will do it."

After that, we called everybody back in and hugged and talked. Naturally, I planned to miss the game and stay with my wife. But a few minutes after one, Valerie said, "Shaun, I'm feeling better."

"Oh, that's good," I said.

"No—I mean I'm okay now. My mom's here, your mom's here, my girl-friends are here, so I'm going to sleep. Shaun, go to the game."

"Are you sure?" I asked.

"I'm sure," she said with a smile.

I took off and hightailed it to the stadium. As I pulled in, some fans who must have heard about the baby cheered me. After I dressed, I went out onto the field, and the crowd erupted in applause.

Our team was down by 10. I ripped off a couple of good runs, and we got going. Matt Hasselbeck quarterbacked, and we ended up having a great game. Matt threw a touchdown pass to Koren Robinson with about two minutes left, and we won—which made us 3 and 0 for the season. It was one of the few times in Seahawk history that the team had started off 3 and 0.

We were pumped—and it was just an awesome day for me. What could be better? My baby girl was born healthy, and our team was 3 and 0.

"This is an amazing way to start the '03 season," I said. "It's an amazing way for a baby to be born."

I'll always remember that day—September 21, 2003—as very, very special.

Chapter 16

A STRONG FOUNDATION

In 2004, my career with the NFL was on track. I had just finished my fourth year. We had made it to the playoffs for the first time in my career, it was my third year starting, and it was my third year with at least 1100 rushing yards and 16 touchdowns. Yet I sensed that bigger and more exciting things were on the horizon. In 2000 I had started the Shaun Alexander Family Foundation to help those in need. But by 2004, Val and I realized we weren't as tightly focused as we needed to be, and we looked for ways to make the foundation more efficient.

"My heart is simple," I told Val. "I want to see young guys grow into great, godly men—men who live in integrity and have good character. I want them to learn to be obedient to the truth. And when they stumble, I want to see them get up, dust themselves off, and jump back in the fight."

So the Shaun Alexander Foundation became committed to teaching younger men how to do just that. In particular, we started doing what we could to remedy the fatherless plague in the United States. In chapter 23 I'll tell you more about what the foundation is now doing, but briefly, our goal is to teach young men that even though their fathers may have failed them or weren't good role models, they still have a job to do. We tell them, "No matter how you were treated by your dad, *you* have to become the role model for others. To do that you need to excel in your studies. Become a great person. Be a classy person. Have integrity."

The goal Val and I have for the foundation harkens back to when I was a kid and—thanks to the inspiring words of my teacher Mrs. Walton—realized that all I had to do was be the best Shaun I could be. That's what I want every kid to know—that they have the potential to do and be far more than they may expect of themselves right now. I want to give them the goal and the confidence to become the best person they can be.

So to help kids achieve this, the foundation began focusing on giving them the tools to cope with life—whether by sending them to a camp, helping them meet the right teacher, or encouraging them when they're down—and on helping them learn to set goals and reach those goals.

◆ ❖ ◆

That year I was also continuing to receive invitations to speak to groups. In June, FCA invited me to Estes Park, Colorado, to speak to a YMCA assembly for an FCA Leadership Conference. At this conference there were about 200 high school boys and an equal number of girls.

Whenever I speak to such groups, I try to share from my heart and offer encouragement for my listeners to seek God and His best for their lives.

As I spoke there at Estes Park, I decided to do something I had often done when I'd led the FCA meetings in Alabama. I told the kids, "I'm going to do something tonight I haven't done in a long time…we're going to do a Jesus cheer." I explained how it worked. They were all athletes, and they caught on immediately.

"Give me a J!" I shouted.

"J!" they roared back. "You've got your J! You've got your J!"

"Give me an E!"

We went through all five letters of Jesus' name before I yelled, "Who is the King?"

"Jesus!" they thundered back.

Then we cheered for Jesus Christ, and I followed up by telling the crowd about my walk with Him. Then I moved to another subject that I often touch on because of its importance to today's youth—and that's the subject of sexual purity.

I felt I had to make sure the students got the message of how God views sexuality: as a gift to men and women to enjoy within a marriage relationship. So I said to the girls, "While I speak to the boys, I'd like all you girls to bow your heads." I waited for a moment for them to do that. Then I addressed the boys: "Okay, guys, I want every one of you to look right at me." I then challenged those boys to stand firm for Jesus Christ and to "stay free from alcohol, drugs, and premarital sex—and whatever temptations face you."

Then I asked the boys to bow their heads while I spoke to the girls. I gave them a similar challenge, encouraging them to stand firm on the same issues. "If you want to marry a prince," I said, "you have to be a godly young lady—a princess worthy of him." I spoke straightforwardly because it's a topic about which I'm passionate.

After that, I asked all of the kids to look directly at me, and I challenged them to rededicate themselves to Jesus Christ. "I'm going to pray for Jesus to help you become godly leaders—to be examples to your peers," I said. After I prayed with them, I spoke to any of them who might not be believers.

"Get up out of your seat right now and go to the back of the room," I said. "We'll meet you there and show you how to let Jesus become the ruler of your life."

I kept speaking, and before long many of those young athletes had walked to the back of the room. When we finished the meeting, I joined the group and asked them to stand in a circle. I then talked to them about what a life commitment to Jesus Christ really means and finished up by praying with them.

The decisions that are made at times like these are turning points in the lives of young people. Their future can literally be at stake as they decide whether to join Christ, be with Him, and enjoy a blessed life here and eternally—or simply wander through life aimlessly, always wondering why things don't go the way they want them to, or feeling lucky that something finally did go right. I'd rather live life knowing that I will eventually be victorious with Jesus than to live life hoping I did enough to win.

To me, having an impact on these kids and helping them build a strong foundation for life is far more rewarding than scoring touchdowns.

Chapter 17

ONE YARD SHORT

In the previous chapter I said that 2004 was on track for me—and it was in all areas of my life. My faith and love for Jesus was growing. My daughter turned one year old, and we found out that baby number two was on the way. The Foundation was becoming focused. And in football my fifth season was finishing strong. With one game left in the regular season, I had more yards and touchdowns than in any previous season in my career. We had already clinched a playoff game, and I was in the lead for the rushing title. With all that, '04 was just an unforgettable year. But the way the season ended put the word "unforgettable" in a whole new light for me.

It all started with me not being careful with my words.

It happened on January 2, 2005, right after the last game of the season against the Atlanta Falcons, and it was reported in the media the next day.

On the morning of January 3, Valerie opened the sports section of the newspaper. After glancing at it, she turned to me and said, "Shaun, I hope you didn't really say that."

She handed me the paper and pointed to a headline with my words: "I was stabbed in the back." At first, I misread it because it didn't compute. I thought it said, "He was stabbed in the back."

I looked at it again, carefully, then leaned over and read the whole article. While the story was partly true, the overall impression it gave was grossly untrue. It had to do with what has been called the "backstabbing incident."

I'd like to tell what really happened. The media painted a picture of me knocking over tables, yelling at coaches and other players, and pouting in a corner. That wasn't true, and I want to set the matter straight. Mostly the issue involved what I was supposed to have said about my coach, Mike Holmgren.

◆ ❖ ◆

To explain everything I have to go back to Wednesday, December 29, four days before we were scheduled to play the Atlanta Falcons. If we won, we'd win the division title and have a playoff game with home-field advantage. The Seahawks hadn't won a playoff game since 1984.

Also, I was about 80 yards away from winning the league rushing title for that year. I knew I was close, but I honestly wasn't thinking much about it. Sure, it's cool to win any title, but that wasn't my goal. I wanted our team to win and for us to have a home game in the playoffs. That was my main concern.

Winning the rushing title seemed like it was a bigger thing for others than it was for me. Our new line coach, Bill Laveroni, said to me, "This is my first year with the Hawks, and my offensive line is going to produce the NFL rushing leader. You're going to win the rushing crown, Shaun."

I laughed and thought, *Bill, you're more excited about this than I am.*

Two of our linemen, Robbie Tobek and Chris Gray, were also fired up. Robbie said, "I might not become a Pro-Bowler, or I might not get all the glitz and glamour like Walter Jones and Steve Hutchinson do, but at least I can say my guy was better than all the others this year." He too was positive I would win the title.

As I listened to them, I wondered if I was making too light of the honor. I realized the rushing title wasn't just a result of something I did—it was a result of the whole team's effort. The guys had pushed a little harder this year, especially when they were tired or hurt. We had won some big games, and now we had a shot at winning the division. The guys were excited about our chance, and their enthusiasm fired me up and made the rushing title more real to me.

We had an excellent pregame practice. We had confidence we would beat the Falcons and go on to the playoffs with the home-field advantage.

During the practice, Mike Holmgren came over to me and gave me a hug. He said, "Shaun, I've had Brett Favre, Steve Young, Joe Montana, and Jerry Rice. They were all great at their positions, but I've never had a guy win the rushing title before." He was pumped. "I'm going to get this for you."

I didn't doubt his word.

Then came game day—Sunday, January 2, 2005. The possibility of winning the rushing title now had me jazzed. As I recall, I needed 83 yards to beat Curtis Martin of the New York Jets, who was in the lead with 1697 yards.

> **At halftime we were leading the Falcons, but I still needed 33 yards...I switched jerseys. That's what we do when a player is close to breaking a mark.**

At halftime we were leading the Falcons, but I still needed 33 yards to beat Curtis. I switched jerseys. That's what we do when a player is close to breaking a mark.

"Thirty-three yards!" one of the guys yelled, and others picked up on it. It was as if the entire line had caught the fever. We went out for the second half, ready to win the game and for me to take the rushing title.

I didn't get the ball often in the third quarter, but I broke a run and figured I was within about 20 yards when the fourth quarter started. Then, with six minutes left in the game, I made a couple of runs that took us up to the goal line. I honestly didn't know for sure, but I figured I was somewhere between five and ten yards away from the title. It was second and goal on the 1-yard line, and we ran a quarterback sneak. Matt Hasselbeck carried for the touchdown that gave us a 28–20 lead.

Atlanta had the ball with four minutes left in the game. We thought our defense would stop them, I'd get the last five yards, we'd win the game, I'd win the rushing title, and everybody would celebrate.

But Atlanta ran the clock down and scored a touchdown on the last play of the game. The score was then 28–26, so they had to try for a two-point conversion to tie and take us into overtime.

Warrick Dunn carried the ball for Atlanta, and he was tackled so close to the goal line that it was hard to tell if he'd actually crossed it. But then the officials ruled he hadn't gotten in. After a review, the call on the field held up—and we won 28–26.

As the game ended I rushed over to Dunn.

"Did you really get in?" I asked, knowing it was hard to tell.

"Naw, I didn't," Warrick said. "Congratulations, Shaun. Good luck in the playoffs."

I could barely hear him, what with the loud cheering and noisy celebrations filling the stadium. The place was just wild with noise. We waved to the fans and gave them high fives. Then I ran back to the middle of the field to take pictures. I also wanted to pray with some of the guys from the other team, as was the custom some of us had at the end of each game.

After the prayer time, I was heading toward the locker room. A reporter stopped me and yelled. "Hey, Shaun—you know you didn't win the rushing title?"

"I figured that," I replied, "because we didn't have any fireworks go off."

"You didn't win the rushing title," he yelled again. "You didn't win the rushing title."

I waved at him as if to say, *Okay, so I didn't win.*

"You only lost by one yard. *One yard.*"

"Really?" I laughed. "Well, we tried."

The reporter wasn't ready to let it go. "You know, it's weird you lost by only one yard. If you go back to your last play, you're on the 1-yard line—and you ran it all the way down there and then they ran a quarterback sneak."

"I never thought of it like that," I said. But I was through talking about it. We had won the game, and that's what counted. I pushed past him.

"Holmgren knew you were only one yard short before he called the play," he yelled as he hurried behind me. Before I could reply, he added, "He kept you from winning the title—and he knew it."

I ignored him, but it planted a seed of doubt in my mind.

"I asked Holmgren about it," the guy went on. "He said he did what he considered to be the best decision."

"Wow!" I said with a chuckle of disbelief. That didn't sound like Mike. I was sure he'd have called a play to help me get the rushing title. "If that's true, he stabbed me in the back," I said to the reporter as I left the field. I held my head high, but inside I was hurt.

During the time between walking off the field and getting into the locker room I had enough time to think about what the reporter had said. Mike had encouraged me. More than once during practice week he'd told me he wanted me to win. Stopping me from winning the title just didn't sound like something he would do.

The first person I saw in the locker room was Heath Evans, one of my closest friends on the team. I said, "You know, that reporter just told me I lost the title by one yard—and that Mike knew it was only one yard and I could have won the title."

Heath shook his head and confirmed what I'd already been thinking. "That doesn't sound like something Mike would do to you."

"Yeah, you're right," I said. And I was ready to forget about it.

Just then one of the players yelled, "Let's go back out and celebrate with the fans."

We all headed back out to the field. It was a great moment for our team. I was high-fived and waved to by fans.

By the time I'd reached the end zone, however, the same reporter had caught up with me again.

"So what do you think?" he asked.

I stared at him blankly.

"Do you really feel stabbed in the back?"

I shrugged my shoulders and kept high-fiving the fans.

I was glad to get rid of the guy. By the time I'd returned to the locker room, shrugged off my equipment, and taken off my football gear, a group of media people had gathered to interview us. One man said loudly, "We hear you feel stabbed in the back. Do you feel stabbed in the back by Mike?"

It was the same reporter.

"Well, yeah," I responded, or something inconsequential like that. I didn't want to talk to him anymore, and I was too naïve to think he was trying to push me into saying something I didn't mean.

That part of the interview lasted all of 30 seconds, and then they were on to other things. It didn't seem like a big deal, or I would have insisted on explaining. The media people went on to ask me maybe 20 questions—typical aftergame stuff. Like always, I smiled and laughed and talked to everyone.

I would learn later that the TV stations broadcast my words but didn't show the video footage. The TV audience never saw my facial expression, so they didn't know the truth—that I had actually made light of the remark.

If they had seen the visuals and the look on my face, they would have concluded, "You can tell Alexander wanted to win, but he's not bent out of shape about the outcome. He's smiling. He doesn't act as if he feels betrayed."

Later the next day, after the whole thing had appeared in the papers, Valerie turned the radio on to a sports talk show. I heard someone say, "We were disappointed with Shaun for trying to make this bigger than it was. He should have been more concerned about the team goal than his own record."

I was offended that the whole situation had been made to seem that way. That's not the type of man I am—it's not the kind of thing I stand for or believe in. Yes, I had said the words, but I wasn't saying them in a malicious way, and I'm positive the reporter knew what I meant. The people who know me understand I don't talk that way. Of course I would have liked to have the rushing title—who wouldn't?—but it wasn't so big that I would bash a man's character over it. The papers had made it sound as if I'd yelled and screamed and made a big, angry scene.

The next day Mike and I talked. He wasn't mad. He explained, "There were so many people around, I didn't know you were only one yard short. I called the play, but I didn't know you were that close."

"Yeah, that sounds more like you." I added, "You already know I wasn't speaking maliciously—I would never do that. You know I'm not like that."

He understood.

I went on. "I wasn't judging you or saying I knew what you were thinking when you called the play. If it had happened the way the reporter said it had and you'd done it deliberately, I would have felt betrayed. I didn't believe you did it intentionally. That was just a figure of speech to the reporter."

An added factor in all of this was that my contract was up with the Seahawks—which I'll say more about in the next chapter. My agent was negotiating with the team, and I was on every network's sports show: ESPN, Fox, ABC, CBS, NBC. On all of them, the same story was running—I had been stabbed in the back. They implied there was trouble between Mike and me or I was unhappy with the Seahawks and wanted to get off the team.

None of that was true.

◆ ❖ ◆

How did the other players look at the incident? They knew me, and they knew Mike. So far as I'm aware, none of them believed it amounted to anything serious.

For example, at our next practice after we had won the game with the Falcons, I walked into the locker room and one of the guys yelled, "Shaun, we hear you're doubtful for the playoffs."

"Doubtful?" I asked. "What do you mean?"

"Yeah—you have serious back wounds."

Everybody laughed.

"Yeah, Shaun, we don't know if we're going to be able to win the next game," someone else yelled, "'cause we don't know when you're going to get out of the hospital."

For several minutes, we cracked jokes and had a good time. The other guys knew it wasn't a big deal. I felt better when I realized that the people who really counted knew the truth.

The rest of the week we trained for the playoff game against the Rams. The stabbed-in-the-back story took attention from the game itself because the media people wouldn't leave it alone. They kept after me with questions like, "Has this affected your team?" "How is your team getting along with the Shaun-and-Mike situation?" "Is this going to cause trauma for Shaun in the future?"

The end of the story is that we lost to the Rams in the playoffs. It's embarrassing to lose a game, but we had lost to them twice during the season already.

I did get a little upset when one reporter said, "Alexander's outbreak in the locker room caused distraction for the team." Maybe that hurt because part of me believes my remarks *were* a distraction. I hadn't answered wisely.

When another reporter brought up the incident later, he asked me, "What would you have done differently?"

"I would probably have gone immediately to Mike," I replied, "and asked him what had happened."

And yet, as I thought more about it later, I realized I probably wouldn't have done that. To me, it wasn't a big issue.

Chapter 18

FRANCHISED

t was Monday, January 7, 2005. The New England Patriots had just won their third Super Bowl in four years, and I was in Hawaii with the family for the Pro Bowl.

It was a weird time for the Seahawks. There were three of us up for contract renewal at the same time. Besides me, there were Walter Jones, our left tackle (and one of the best in football), and Matt Hasselbeck, our quarterback. It was possible for Seattle to re-sign all three of us. The question was how.

Walt, Matt, and I were all in Hawaii to play in the Pro Bowl. While I was there for that game, a number of players from other teams were in my ear, telling me things like:

"Play with us because we can do more for you."

"You think it's great over there in Seattle? Give us a chance to show you how you can *really* stand out."

"You join our team, and we'll get you to the Super Bowl."

"You'll take us to the Super Bowl because you're the one piece of the puzzle we're missing."

It felt exciting to be courted by those other teams, promising me how happy my wife and daughter would be if I signed with them.

There was also another side—the negative side. The players would try to put a lot of doubt in my mind by saying stuff like, "You're a great player, but Seattle hasn't treated you right. Come with us, and we'll treat you right."

Another said, "Shaun, you're the best running back in the NFL, and they act like you're not working hard. The stats say you're the best."

From that time and on into March, I moved between elation and confusion. The Seahawks signed Walter while we were still in Hawaii; they signed Matt the first of March; and finally, they franchised me. This meant they were offering me a short-term contract to play for one year for the average salaries of the top five NFL players, which was around $6.3 million.

> If God was with me and in charge of my life, I had nothing to worry about. It's easy to say that when everything is going the way you want it. But now I had to wait—and trust. That's when it's the hardest.

I smiled when I heard that figure. When I thought about how I'd been raised in a two-bedroom apartment, which we didn't even own, I figured I could handle a one-year deal for $6.3 million. When I was growing up, if we had a hundred dollars we were happy.

Of course, I was now in the professional ranks, where most of us play less than ten years. We work hard for a few years and then our professional days are behind us. During those years, the dollar amounts are staggering, but they represent a career's worth of pay in the NFL.

Until the contract issues came up, I had rarely thought about being underpaid. But after I talked to various team reps, other players, and even a couple of agents, I came to realize that what others were telling me was correct—when compared with that of other running backs, my compensation was lower.

I received a lot of well-meaning advice: "Hold out." "Don't sign the deal." "You deserve more." "Make them pay—you deserve better." "They should treat you better. You're a great guy, and you're an asset in the community."

Constantly people came to me, and it seemed like their sentences all began the same way: "You deserve…You deserve…"

I tried not to let their voices push me into rash decisions. Meanwhile Valerie and I prayed a lot and waited for God to show me what to do.

I learned many important things during this time. I could have agreed with the people who spoke against the Seahawks and complained about my treatment. I could have sulked because Walter and Matt had received contracts and I hadn't.

Instead, I said nothing.

Every time I prayed for God's guidance, the answer came back the same: "Sit still and know that I am God."

That was a test of my faith, but it was also a powerful experience for me. If God was with me and in charge of my life, I had nothing to worry about. It's easy to say that when everything is going the way you want it. But now I had to wait—and trust. That's when it's the hardest.

But I did trust...and wait...and wait...and wait.

Valerie and I kept on praying earnestly, and God gave us peace.

Something else was going on in our lives at this time. Valerie was pregnant again and, looking ahead to the new addition to our family, we began thinking about our need for a larger house. We had a small but nice home. It had been perfect for me as a bachelor before we married. But more than that, Val and I wanted *our* place. We decided we'd probably have a third child eventually, and we also wanted room for guests. So we felt we'd like four or five bedrooms, as well as a nice yard for the kids to play in.

We decided that if God provided us with a new house—just the kind we wanted—we'd know it was His plan for me to remain with the Seahawks.

So we contacted a real estate agent, and the woman drove us around the areas where we said we'd like to live. We saw a large number of fine houses. The problem was the price—they were all more than we wanted to pay.

I couldn't believe it. After having grown up in an apartment, I wasn't willing to spend *that* much for a house.

So we prayed.

In the book of Habakkuk it says to write down the vision and then wait for God to make it happen. Taking this to heart, Valerie and I wrote down what we wanted in a house. Here is what we prayed: "God, if it's Your will for us to stay in Seattle, You will make it happen. If You provide the kind of house we ask for, we'll know this is Your will."

We talked a long time to decide exactly what kind of house would make us both content. We agreed on seven things, so we wrote them down and prayed about them:

1. We decided exactly how much money we would spend.
2. We decided on the general location where we wanted to live.
3. We agreed that we wanted at least eight-tenths of an acre of land.
4. We included the accommodations we wanted inside the house.
5. We wanted a guest section separate from the house.
6. We wanted to have a sports court.
7. And a final important item: We felt we had to have a privacy gate so people couldn't just walk up to the house. As our kids got older, we didn't want that.

On March 15 we took the list to our real estate agent, read it to her, and told her how much we were willing to pay.

She laughed. "You'll never find all these things for that price."

We didn't argue with her. We knew what we wanted, and we were willing to trust God to provide. Back home, Val prayed, "God, now You get to go to work."

That's when we added an eighth item to our list. We wrote the date of April 1. By that, we were indicating that God would provide the house by April 1—which was only two weeks away.

We prayed, we believed, and we rested. We sincerely believed God was going to work on our behalf.

On the morning of April 1, Valerie called me in New York. I had flown there to meet with a good friend, a rapper named Draze. Val told me she'd been invited to go to a yard sale the next day by Dr. Deb, our chiropractor.

The next morning at the yard sale, Valerie overheard two women talking. One of them said she and her husband were planning to move out of their house because they wanted to downsize.

Valerie knew the woman and asked her, "You're selling your house? Can you tell me about the place?"

The woman described it. "Where we are now is eight-tenths of an acre," she said. "We have a separate guest section…" As Valerie listened, the woman went right down the list of the seven items we wanted. Val knew God had answered our prayer. Instead of blurting that out, however, she asked calmly, "Can I go with you and look at the house?"

The woman was delighted to do it even though they hadn't yet put the house on the market. They drove there and Valerie did a walk-through. Then she stepped outside and called me in New York and told me, "Shaun, I'm standing in front of our new home."

Then she went back inside and told the woman, "My husband is out of town but he'll be back tomorrow. When he's back, can we talk about the house?"

She agreed.

I flew back to Seattle, and the next day Val and I went over to the house. Because I knew the area, I'd seen it from the outside. Valerie described the inside and was so excited that she said, "I don't care what the price is—let's get it."

"No," I reminded her, "we wrote down a price."

"You're right," she replied. "But I sure hope God wants us to have that house!"

If that was truly the case, we both knew we would get it for the price we had written down.

After we had walked through the house and I'd agreed that I liked it too, I met with the husband. We were sitting across the table from each other—and on a slip of paper, I had written the amount we wanted to pay. I also knew the house was worth much more than I planned to offer. My faith had already started to shake a little because I knew Val wanted the house so badly.

"How much do you want for it?" I finally asked.

He told me the price. And then I handed him the paper on which I had written the price. It was exactly the amount he had named.

"This is our house, then," I said.

He was floored because he thought it was going to take him a long time to sell. And we had made an offer before he'd even put the house on the market, which was supposed to happen April 5.

"God is at work!" Val and I kept saying to each other. "God is at work!"

We had the house, and it met all our qualifications. And we had been led to it through that phone call from Dr. Deb inviting Valerie to go to the yard sale—on April 1, our deadline.

We set the date for the closing and made plans to move in on July 15, 2005.

We still had one problem: I had not yet signed a contract with the Seahawks. But I was at peace, and so was Val. I'd finished my traveling and speaking commitments, and we hadn't said anything to anyone about moving. We decided to keep it quiet until after the contract was signed.

That same day—July 15—would be the end of my free agency. That's the period during which players with expired contracts can look for new jobs. After that, the Seahawks would be allowed to offer me a long-term contract or I could sign the one-year franchise offer. There are players who hold out until right before the start of the season or even miss the first couple of games in order to get a better deal.

One more factor in all this: Our second baby was due within three weeks after our move, and we wanted to have everything ready in the new house by the time the baby arrived. I specifically prayed, "Okay, God, You got me. We bought this new house and I know You're working something out, and we're going to believe for that. I still haven't received a contract, but I believe this waiting is also part of Your plan."

Normally, I would have been anxious and been on the phone every day to my agent, but Val and I remained absolutely calm. We felt God would work on our behalf.

I get CDs and books all the time from people who think they know what's going on in my life and try to cheer me up or encourage me (or sometimes set me straight). Right around that time, though, I received a teaching CD from Brian McCormack, one of the young men I mentor. Brian had gone with me several times when I'd spoken in various places. The CD he sent me was about being content.

I looked at it for several seconds and then thought, *I need to hear this.* A few friends had already urged me to be content with the franchise tag. More than one had said something like, "Shaun, it's $6.3 million. How could that not be enough?" They thought I was holding out for a better deal. But I wasn't doing anything but waiting for divine directions. They didn't realize (and Val and I didn't try to tell them) that we were content to wait.

I put on the CD from Brian. Three times the speaker asked, "What if things don't go the way you want them to go? Will you still be obedient?"

After the speaker asked that question for the third time, I started to listen carefully. I closed my eyes in prayer and talked to God. Valerie and I wanted to stay in Seattle, but we also wanted to be content to move. That was the one area where I still felt some anxiety. I didn't *want* to move, though I was *willing* to move. Our location was more important to me than the money issue.

I realized that was the last thing I needed to surrender to God. Finally, I said, "Lord, I'd be content even if I couldn't stay in Seattle—and if You don't want us to stay here, I'm ready to move. I'll go wherever You want me to go. I know that wherever I am I can reach out to young men and help them grow. I know You'll make my family and me happy no matter where we live." I paused and said as sincerely as I knew how, "If You're calling us to become servants in another city, I'll be content."

Something happened to me just then. I *had* been content, but now a deeper level of peace and contentment took control of my life. It seemed as if Bible verses rushed through my head, assuring me everything was all right. I was at that place where I was so content that I honestly didn't care what happened with the house or the Seahawks. God was with me. That was all that mattered.

I had been studying in the book of Genesis and had finished the portion about God's promise to Abraham of a son and an heir through whom he would have many, many descendants. Because of their impatience with God, who didn't seem to be fulfilling His promise, Sarah and Abraham took matters into their own hands. Sarah couldn't have children, so she talked Abraham into having a child with Hagar, her servant woman.

Hagar then bore Abraham a son named Ishmael. It seemed natural that he would be Abraham's heir and the one through whom the promised multitudes of descendants would come.

For the next 13 years, Ishmael was raised as if he would be the heir. During those years, Abraham taught him how to be a man of God and to obey, and how to respect others—but most of all, I assume, to be his heir.

Then—25 years after God had first promised Abraham a son and 13 years after Ishmael's birth—Sarah conceived, even though she was well past childbearing age, and bore Isaac. Immediately, with Isaac's birth, Ishmael's inheritance was snatched from him.

After I had read that section, I thought, *According to most people, Ishmael had the right to be upset. He had the right to say to Abraham, "You're my father, even though the slave woman is my mother. You trained me and taught me for 13 years."*

> **I understood then. The attitude of the team's owners was not the issue. God was in control. The big choice was how I would react.**

I saw how that related to my own situation. I had played well and had been a good investment for my team. They had given contracts to everyone except me. According to others, I had every right to be discontent. In fact, some people suggested to me that I should be angry. Some expected me to blast the team and call in the media and tell them what a bad deal I had received.

I couldn't do that because I was trusting God to provide for me. If my life truly belonged to God, it was His responsibility to intervene for me.

I continued to think about Hagar and Ishmael. They would have been justified in their anger. Hagar could have screamed, "Sarah, you made me volunteer my body to your husband, Abraham. I bore him a son named Ishmael. Abraham, you raised Ishmael for 13 years to be the heir. And then you took it all away. That's wrong."

I could easily argue that Hagar and Ishmael deserved better. In my own situation, I could make the same argument.

But no matter what we think we deserve, we still have to make choices. Ishmael should have accepted what God had for his life. He should just have gotten in line with God's plan.

But Ishmael didn't. He had the wrong attitude, and mocked Isaac to the point that eventually Abraham kicked Ishmael and his mother out. They lost because they didn't have the right attitude.

I said to myself, "Shaun, you know what? You have every right to be upset. You've been paid hundreds of thousands of dollars when you should have received millions. By all the logic of the world around you, you should yell, 'I'm not going to stand for this.'"

But I couldn't do that. It was as if God spoke and said, *You choose, Shaun. You can choose to build a team of humility, selflessness, sacrifice, and love—or you can take the negative path. You can mock, argue, become bitter, and spread gossip about the coaches and the owners. It's your choice.*

I understood then. The attitude of the team's owners was not the issue. God was in control. The big choice was how I would react.

As I sat there in silence, I knew I wanted to help build a strong team. I wanted to have fun and crack jokes with other players. I wanted us to win. I made my decision to accept the franchise and stay in Seattle. I would go to training camp.

I walked into the other part of the house and said to Valerie, "Sweetie, I've got something to tell you."

Before I could tell her she said, "Shaun, I feel like you're supposed to go to training camp." She knew too.

It was July 25, and training camp started three days later, on July 28.

Not only had God spoken to me, but He had spoken to Valerie at the same time. I told her about my meditation on the story of Ishmael and Hagar. "It's a choice," I said. "I might have to get in line with God's plan. I may be wrong but..."

"You're not wrong," she assured me. "You're *right*."

I decided to call my agents and tell them I was willing to go to training camp, even though I knew my friends would think I had caved in from the pressure. One friend said, "If you just hold out, they'll lose four or five of their first games. Then they'll realize how big your talent is, and they'll offer you millions of dollars."

I didn't argue. I simply said, "I've chosen to go, and I'm going to stick with it." My friend meant well, but I knew what God wanted me to do.

My agents from SFX Sports Group contacted the owners and said I would attend training camp. The Seahawks told them, "If Shaun agrees to play for $6.3 million this year, we'll promise not to franchise him next year."

And that is the deal I signed.

Chapter 19

A SPECIAL BLESSING

We moved into our new house on July 15. On July 25, I agreed to the Seahawks' terms. On July 27, I signed the contract, which stated I would play for one year for $6.3 million with a guarantee I wouldn't be franchised the following year. On July 28, training camp would start.

I didn't realize my plans would be pleasantly interrupted.

The evening of July 27, I began to pack before going to bed. About four o'clock in the morning Valerie shook me and said, "Shaun, I'm in a lot of pain." She didn't need to explain that the contractions had started.

While I packed the car, the intensity of Valerie's contractions was increasing. If I didn't show up at camp, I wasn't worried that the team would think I had backed out. The Seahawks have always recognized that family issues take precedence in a case like this. Our baby was coming, and I was going to be there.

A doctor attended Heaven's birth, but we had decided on a midwife the second time. So I drove Valerie to the midwife's office, which is a kind of birthing center. Almost as soon as we arrived, the midwife ran a warm bath to help Valerie relax.

She eased into the bath and tried to relax a little, but I could tell the pain from the contractions had intensified. She stayed in the tub for maybe 45 minutes and then climbed out, dried off, and went to bed. She was ready to deliver.

And at 9:28 AM on July 28, 2005, our second daughter, Trinity Monet Alexander, was born. It was such a wonderful and tender moment for me. I took Trinity into my arms and prayed for her. Even at birth she was different from Heaven, and I knew already she would have her own distinct personality.

After the delivery Valerie rested, and at noon I called my agents and asked them to let the Seahawks know about Trinity's birth. I was going to stay with my wife for a couple of days, but I wanted to make sure the team knew the reason I would be late.

Valerie and Trinity stayed at the midwife's office for two hours before I took them home. Then Momma Boyd came and stayed with us for a month to help, and she was a huge blessing to us.

Life was going so well for us now—but I didn't realize God was ready for it to become even better.

Chapter 20

THE BIG SEASON

When I arrived at training camp—two days late because of the birth of Trinity—the other players gathered around and welcomed me back. We had bonded like a family, and we were determined to have a great season.

One of the first things we did was to set goals. The enthusiasm we developed was contagious—we were the most energized I'd ever seen the team. Typical of the comments were these:

"We won't win the rushing title by just one yard—let's go blow the thing out of the water."

"Let's break all kinds of records this year. Let's get our team to the Super Bowl and win."

"Let's do things our city has never seen before."

Since their inaugural season in 1976, the Seahawks had never been to the Super Bowl. We determined to change that in the 2005/2006 season.

People in the press have since asked, "What kind of pressure did you feel?"

The truth? I didn't feel any personal pressure. If we had been playing in a card game, I would have said to them, "God is the dealer, and He's already stacked the deck on my side." I truly felt that way.

So we left camp on a high note—and I felt even more positive that my decision to accept the franchise contract and stay with Seattle was the right one.

This was also confirmed by Tim Ruskell, the newly hired president of the Seahawks. The first time we met, he admitted, "Shaun, I don't know much about you." He knew the stats, of course. He also knew about the infamous "backstabbing" incident. He explained he wanted to watch me, get to know me, and see me on and off the field. Then he gave me a big smile and said, "I promise you that if you have a great year, you'll be more than happy with what happens next year."

I took him at his word.

One of the best changes in the new season was that Mike Holmgren was freed from other responsibilities besides coaching. From 1999 until 2005, Mike had had many jobs. He had been part of the committee that decided our salaries, drafted the college players, and traded current players. But after Tim came on board as president, they hired a couple of other people to take on those responsibilities, and Mike's only job was coaching.

That was one more factor that solidified the team. I'd always liked Mike, but I liked him even better when he talked to me just as a head coach instead of having to mix in the responsibilities of all the other titles he had previously filled.

Like any great coach, Mike is tough on all his players. That's what makes him excel. So even before we played our first game our team was the most prepared and cohesive it had ever been. We hadn't always been like that.

For example, in previous years guys would miss practice. And they would be late to the airport, late to meetings, and even late to games. Sure, they had reasons—"Sorry, coach, but I overslept." Those past Seahawks teams were full of excuses. This team was different. This was a new season. We were focused and excited to play together.

Something else made the cohesiveness even clearer to me: The entire team began to hang out together off the field. I hadn't seen that happen before, but now we wanted to be with each other both on and off the field. As a result, we became even closer—we knew each other better than we had before. We wanted to be champions—and we had taken the first step toward that goal: We became a team.

◆ ❖ ◆

We lost the first game of the season, which was against Jacksonville, but we won the next two. In our fourth game we played the Redskins—and in overtime, they kicked a field goal and beat us.

After that loss, we had an 11-game winning streak. Game after game, we beat our opponents. We were pumped. It was our best season yet, and all of us were starting to set our eyes on the Super Bowl.

My attitude about winning and losing depends a lot on what part of the season it is. At the beginning, we always have new members on the team, and even those of us who are seasoned players have been apart for months. We're still trying to feel out how our team works together on the field. We know from our first games the things we need to do differently.

In the game against Jacksonville, our defense played extremely well—in fact, I think it was one of the best defensive games I've seen us play since I've been a Seahawk. I told the media people, "We lost this game, but if our defense plays like this the rest of the year, we're going to steamroll the other teams."

I was right. I saw aggressiveness and determination in the faces of my teammates. We were simply stronger and more motivated than ever before. Those guys made plays I didn't think I would ever see them make. So often in the past, we had stopped teams from doing things because *they* made mistakes. That was no longer true. Now we stopped them because *we* did things exactly right. Our defense was steamrolling. Our offense was also on fire, and we were all playing our best.

Because of that smooth flow, I was able to have some unbelievable games. I scored four touchdowns in one game and three in another. Our great performances on the field resulted in huge support among our fans. That was the most excitement I'd ever seen in the city of Seattle.

We were ready to play against the Green Bay Packers in the last game of the season. At that time, I was in the lead for the rushing title by about 100 yards and I had scored 27 touchdowns, which tied the NFL record.

And that's when I experienced a personal bump in the road.

Chapter 21

BREAKING RECORDS, MAKING THE PLAYOFFS

It was late Christmas night, just before midnight, when Durran called with the news. Our Aunt Debbie—my mother's younger sister, whom I loved dearly, had passed. She had been diabetic for years before they had diagnosed her with a skin virus. Her last months were very painful. I felt close to all my mother's family, so it was a big loss for me.

I flew home for the funeral, which was held in Cincinnati. It was a mixture of joy and sadness at seeing all my family again as we faced the loss of Aunt Debbie. Our family decided to call it a homecoming party instead of a funeral. We wanted to celebrate her life instead of just mourn her death. At the service and afterward, family members and friends shared touching stories about the wonderful woman Debbie had been.

As I listened to their tributes, it made me happy to hear of the positive impact she had made on others. I knew how much she had meant to me. I thought of her influence on my own life. Tears came to my eyes as I realized the loss. *She's really gone,* I said to myself several times. It was hard for me to believe. A very sad time.

◆ ❖ ◆

I came home from the funeral emotionally drained. Nevertheless I had to leave the next morning for the upcoming game in Green Bay. At this point, I was closing in on two records: the '05 rushing title and the number of touchdowns in a single season.

When I checked into my room at the hotel in Green Bay, I turned on the TV to see that Tiki Barber of the Giants had just made a 95-yard run in their game that day. That meant he had passed me in total yards rushing. I would need about 40 yards to win the rushing title.

During the first half of the Green Bay game, Mike Holmgren called plays that gave me the ball in just about every down. On one drive, we moved down to the goal line and called 17 G-lead, which is a running play to the left. Matt handed me the ball, and I ran for the corner and walked in.

"Touchdown Alexander!" the announcer yelled.

The crowd went crazy. It had been only a one-yard run, but it gave me the twenty-eighth touchdown—which meant I held the record for the most touchdowns in an NFL season.

As I came to the sidelines, some of the players danced around, grabbed me, and shouted. From everywhere around me I heard people congratulating me. The guys from the offensive line seemed to be as excited as I was. Everyone was pumped, and it was a great moment for me.

As soon as it quieted down, Mike walked over to me and said, "Okay, we've got to give you some yards now."

He gave me the ball several times again, and I ended up breaking the record for rushing. I finished the season with 1880 yards rushing and a record total of 28 touchdowns.

Even after I got those rushing yards and the record-breaking touchdown, we still lost the game. Our coach took all the starters out so we played only with our backups. We played to win, but it wasn't with our guns blazing—so we lost. But then, that's football.

We closed the season with a great record—13 wins and 3 losses. We had made the NFL playoffs, and we would play in Seattle, giving us the home-field advantage.

Our only serious loss during the regular season had been to the Washington Redskins—and guess who we were to face in the playoff game? Yep, it was the Redskins.

That was a rough week for me. My daughter Heaven had been sick with a viral flu during the week before the game. Then I became sick—*really* sick—after catching it from her.

My ears were clogged, and I couldn't breathe through my nose. My throat was unbelievably sore. I was nauseous and had terrible stomachaches—just what Heaven had gone through.

I just don't take medicine of any kind, so I tried to rely on water, lemons, and throat lozenges to do the job. But they didn't help much. I kept telling myself, "I'll be okay...I'll throw this off," but I didn't.

> **I took all three medications...Now I not only felt bad from the virus, but I also felt dopey—so much so that before the game I fell asleep in the locker room with all my gear on.**

I went to our practices, but I felt really bad and didn't practice well at all.

On Saturday before the game, I didn't do the walk-throughs. I was shaking badly and couldn't stop.

But the plain fact was, we were in the playoffs. The team needed me, and I needed to be out on the field. I realized I couldn't get out there and play without help, so the night before the game, I gave in and took some medicine. I don't remember what the pills were, but there were three kinds. One was supposed to kill the virus, but the side effect was that it clogged me up and gave me a headache. The second fixed the headache but made my eyes water and my nose run. And the third fixed all the symptoms but made me sleepy.

I took all three medications again the morning of the game. By the time I arrived at the stadium, I was almost completely out of it. Now I not only felt bad from the virus, but I also felt dopey—so much so that before the game I fell asleep in the locker room with all my gear on. At the last moment I snapped awake and went out with the team.

As we were coming out of the tunnel, I leaned over to Matt and said, "Didn't you think the crowd would be a little bit louder?"

"You're kidding, right?" he said.

I then realized the problem wasn't with the crowd—I just wasn't able to hear very well. I didn't want anyone to know how bad I felt, so I put on a silly grin and laughed it off.

The game started. On my second carry, we ran a play to the left. I was behind Walter Jones and Steve Hutchinson. They usually do a really good job just blocking and making a big hole for me. I then cut back to the right—and my knee knocked the football out of my hands. I fumbled it on the ten-yard line. Though the ball was right there in front of me, I didn't jump on it. I just didn't know what was going on. I was hoping it was just the drugs.

On the next drive, Matt handed me the ball and I ran to the left, and then turned and dove forward for more yards. I don't remember anything after that. Afterward, I learned that someone's forearm hit me in the back of the head and knocked me out.

I had a concussion—the first I've ever had. When I was awake enough to realize what was going on, I was seated on the bench. I couldn't figure how I'd gotten there. I looked to the left, and the linemen were missing. I looked on the Jumbotron and saw Matt getting ready to throw a pass. I asked myself, *What's going on?* I saw the guys on the field, but nothing made any sense.

I must have looked pretty dazed because the next thing I knew the doctor was standing in front of me and asking, "Do you remember getting knocked out?"

I just looked around.

He told me, "Shaun, you were out for about 20 minutes."

I couldn't believe it.

The hit had been a heavy one, but I think it was worse because of the medicines I had taken. I think I'd been ready to fall asleep and the hit just finished me off.

As soon as I felt fully awake, I began to pray for God to restore me. I've often told people how powerful prayer is, and I experienced the effects right then. The doctors were amazed.

I knew friends who were watching the game were praying for me. I also knew soon that God had answered our prayers. I didn't get to go back into the game, but I did get to feeling more like myself. Not fully—but at least I knew what was going on around me.

We won the game. The crowd roared, and all of us on the team were jubilant. This was the Seahawks' first playoff win since 1984. This was what we had worked for all season. We had achieved our goal.

◆ ❖ ◆

The next day I met with the team doctor. After he'd examined me, I said, "I feel a lot better today than I did yesterday."

"That's good," he said. "How do you feel? What percentage?"

"About 80 percent," I said.

He laughed. "No, Shaun, you're not 80 percent."

I didn't argue, but the next day I went back to see him. I felt better than I had the day before. I said, "I feel better today, so I think I'm really about 80 percent normal this time."

"Why do you say that?" he asked.

"I know I'm not 100 percent yet," I said, "but I definitely think I'm about 80."

He shook his head. "No, Shaun—you're still not 80 percent."

By Wednesday I felt a definite physical boost. I was improving every day, but I must have started very low. I can honestly say that concussions are weird, but prayers are powerful. Every day I felt much better than the day before. I wasn't totally normal yet, but I felt all right.

◆ ❖ ◆

It was Sunday again, and we were ready to go out and play the Carolina Panthers for the NFC Championship.

It had now been a week since the concussion, and the doctor released me to play. He did ask, "How do you feel?"

"Good," I said. "Just make sure no one hits me in the head."

One of guys in the locker room laughed and yelled, "How are you going to be a running back and not get hit in the head?"

"Good point," I said and smiled. When I gave him that comeback, I knew I was all right again.

On the first play of the game, one of the Panther safeties blitzed and hit me smack in the face. Not only was I hit, but I fell over the legs of one of my linemen and landed flat on my rear end.

I'm all right. That was the first thing that ran through my mind. I jumped to my feet. I didn't want anyone to think I might have had a repeat of the previous week's injury.

I not only felt fine but I was ready to play again. I finished the game with 132 yards rushing and two touchdowns.

Even better, we won the game—and we were headed to our first Super Bowl!

After the game, it was a wonderful experience to stand on the platform while they brought out our trophies. Paul Allen, Tim Ruskell, Mike Holmgren, Matt Hasselbeck, and I made speeches. We could hardly contain our excitement. This would be our first trip to the Super Bowl in team history. That was the fact that was on everyone's mind.

We were rolling—on our way to Detroit to play against the Pittsburgh Steelers.

We were so excited!

Super Bowl!

◆ ❖ ◆

Chapter 22

MVP AND
SUPER BOWL XL

One day near the end of the season, we were getting ready to practice when Moe Kelly (our director of player development) walked by me and signaled a thumbs-up. Seconds later, Mike Holmgren held up his hand for us to stop talking. Then he called out, "We have an announcement. This year's MVP is—Shaun Alexander."

It was a special moment, followed by a lot of clapping, hugs, and congratulations from my teammates.

Here's how the award works. Sportswriters of the Associated Press—50 of them, I think—pick the player they believe is the best one that year in the NFL. I heard I received 19 of those votes.

Not only was I the first running back to win the MVP award since 2000, but I was the first player to do so in the Seahawks' history.

The MVP Award was the culmination of a truly great season—two records for me and the Seahawks' first trip to the Super Bowl.

To receive the MVP *is* an honor. It's great publicity for the player himself, his team, and for the NFL. The MVP award winner is given a huge trophy, and receives a lot of press coverage and numerous invitations to special dinners.

Then it's over.

My philosophy is that the players who receive the MVP award, like me, don't truly appreciate it until *after* we've left the game. It's an experience we can look back on and say, "I was the best player that year. Those were the good times." But while we're still in the midst of our careers, we're always looking ahead to that next season and its unique challenges. Or the next record to be broken. There really isn't much time to reflect on our achievements while they're happening. Great players are always hungry for the next achievement.

What am I hungry for now?

I want to win the MVP Award a second time, a third time…and maybe even a fourth time! Other running backs have won it—great players like Jim Brown, Barry Sanders, and Marshall Faulk. But no running back has ever won it two years in a row. I'd like to be the first to do that.

After our win against Carolina, we had two weeks to get ready. Two weeks until our trip to Detroit and the biggest game the Seahawks had ever played.

The site for each Super Bowl is supposed to be neutral. But Detroit is a lot closer to Pittsburgh than it is to Seattle, and that built enthusiasm for the Steelers. Besides that, one of their best players, Jerome Bettis, comes from Detroit. So it was almost like we were playing on Pittsburgh's home field.

The whole event was strange all the way. It was a great honor just to be able to play, but I felt like the odds had been stacked against us. Every commentator called us the underdogs.

We were still pushing to win…then things began to go wrong.

First, we had an incident on the way to do some interviews. On Tuesday night before the game, six of us—Matt Hasselbeck, Walter Jones, Steve Hutchinson, Michael Boulware, Chuck Darby, and I rode together from our hotel to the media location.

With that many starting players in one vehicle, Matt made the comment, "Hey, in case we get in a wreck, we'll have messed up our whole team."

We all laughed and joked about it.

Super Bowl

The National Football League is divided into two conferences, the American Football Conference (AFC) and the National Football Conference (NFC). Each conference contains sixteen teams, divided into four divisions (east, west, north, and south) of four teams each, even though they don't fully correspond to the geographic parts of the country. Seattle is in the west division of the NFC.

A regular season for a team is 16 games. The NFL schedules about 256 games in a season. Each team plays the clubs in its own division twice—once at home and once at the other team's stadium. When the season is over, there is a playoff tournament in which the qualifying teams match up against each other in a series of games. Whichever team wins moves on to the next game. When a team loses in the playoffs, its season is over.

Six teams in both the AFC and NFC make the playoffs; the winners of each division make the playoffs, and two wild-card teams with the next-best records also play. Teams with the best win-loss record in their division win their division.

The first week of the playoffs is called the wild-card round and features the two wild-card teams plus the division winners that had the worst two records of the four division winners. The two division winners that had the best records in each conference get a bye (they don't have to play that first week of the playoffs). They are rewarded for an outstanding season by not having to risk elimination in the first game at home—against the winner of one of the games from the wild-card round.

The intensity level of playoff games goes up because the closer a team gets to the Super Bowl, the more they want to get there. Teams continue to play each other until there are only two teams left—a champion of the NFC and one in the AFC. Those two champions meet in the Super Bowl. There are two weeks between the conference championship game and the Super Bowl.

At the end of it all, it comes down to *one* game: the Super Bowl. Unlike other sports, the entire championship depends on a single game—one super game.

The AFC champs play the NFC champs at a neutral site. Each player on the winning team receives a valuable and prestigious Super Bowl ring, and the team is awarded the Vince Lombardi Trophy—a regulation-size silver football mounted in a kicking position.

As we drove along, we talked about the game. We were really pumped up about it. One of our guys said, "They just don't know how good we are." That was the attitude we'd had all year, and we never got tired of reminding each other of it.

Then Matt mentioned the TV series called *24*. He said something about a secret van and then asked, "What would happen if a missile came in and blew up the van in front of us the way it happened on *24*?" We laughed and came up with silly answers.

Just then we arrived at the security gate that led into the garage. The gate rose to allow the van in front of us to drive in. Our driver started forward, but immediately the gate came down. Two poles that were designed to stop vehicles from trying to rush the gate shot up from the ground and hit the front of the car.

Ordinarily I wear a seat belt, but that time I didn't. Just before we started to move through the gate I had turned sideways to talk to Walter and Hutch—and with the impact, my knees hit the radio, and my face and shoulder struck the dashboard. If we had been going faster, I could have gone through the front window.

Matt bounced back sideways, and all of us were jolted around. It wasn't serious enough to send us to the hospital but we all felt shaken.

Just before we went inside, Hutch said, "Don't any of you give Pittsburgh any comfort—you know what I mean? We're all fine, and we don't want anyone to say anything. He was only driving four miles an hour."

We agreed. "Okay, just four miles an hour. It's not a big deal."

> We laughed about the incident. When one of the trainers asked, "What was the driver wearing?" I replied, "I don't remember—but I'm sure he had a Pittsburgh shirt on underneath."

None of us were hurt badly, but even if we had been, we would have tried to make it sound as insignificant as possible. We had no idea what spin the media might put on it if they heard about it.

We went into the press conference and, sure enough, somebody asked, "Tell us about the fender bender you guys just got into. Is everybody all right?"

"We're fine. No big deal," Walter said.

"It wasn't that big of a deal," Hutch repeated.

"It was a shock," I said, "but we're all okay."

"What are you guys talking about?" a reporter asked.

We laughed.

"It was the dumbest thing we've ever done," Matt said, "I don't know what the driver was thinking."

However, somewhere in the interview the word "wreck" was used, and that gave the media a new angle for their Super Bowl story. So for the next two days they went into a frenzy over the accident.

After we finished the press conference and were ready to leave, we learned that FBI agents had been assigned to escort us from then on—"for our protection," we were told.

"Our protection?" I asked. "Protection from what?" It was unbelievable.

Back at our hotel while we were being checked over, we laughed about the incident. When one of the trainers asked, "What was the driver wearing?" I replied, "I don't remember—but I'm sure he had a Pittsburgh shirt on underneath."

Actually, we felt bad for the driver. He had definitely been excited to drive us around, and because he ended up in a minor wreck, they fired him.

Someone said, "I can just hear Coach Holmgren when he hears about this." Mike had been at a banquet. We laughed as we tried to imagine what it would have been like if someone had rushed to his table and said, "Your quarterback, your tailback, your two Pro Bowl offensive linemen, your number-one safety, and your veteran tackle have all been in a car wreck."

I don't know what they did tell Mike, but I know I would have been upset. It hadn't been easy for us to win our way to the Super Bowl and we would need every player to be at his best. Sure enough, when Mike arrived at the hotel, he was obviously upset.

Mike walked into our training room and asked, "Where's the driver?"

We told him he had already been fired.

"Can I still meet with the guy?" Mike asked.

The guy had already left, and it was just as well…It would have been a really bad night for him if Mike had seen him.

We laughed again, but Mike still looked upset. Before he let us go, he asked each of us, "How are you feeling?"

I just said, "Oh, I'm good." I wasn't going to show him any stiffness. We were fine and ready to get focused for the rest of the week.

On Saturday, the day before the game, we went to Ford Field, the stadium where we'd be playing our biggest game. The billboards in the stadium had all kinds of pro-Pittsburgh statements on them. That made it clear that, instead of being a neutral place, Detroit was definitely for the Steelers.

One sign read, "Shaun Alexander, one carry, negative two yards rushing." And next to it was one that read, "Jerome Bettis, six carries, 70 yards rushing, two touchdowns." All the signs and posters were there to make our players look bad, even though a Super Bowl stadium is supposed to be a neutral place.

Another thing—during the game, the Steelers fans waved yellow towels—which has a long tradition. We saw a few green or white towels wave for us, but only a few. We found out that the vendors kept the yellow towels displayed on the counter, but if fans wanted to buy a Seahawks towel they had to ask for them. Vendors kept them under the counter or would say, "I'll have to go into the back room and get one."

Even though I think that was wrong, ultimately everything comes back to the field. We felt the referees made some bad calls, but they did their best. Our defense played well—however, our offense wasn't as good as we had been all season. We made a couple of mistakes—the kinds we hadn't made all season.

All those factors together resulted in our losing the Super Bowl. During the regular season, our team had averaged just under 28 points per game; in the Super Bowl we lost 21–10. We missed two field goals. Our kicker is one of the top five in the NFL, but that day he missed two attempts. Though they were both 50-yard kicks and most kickers can't make a field goal from that distance, our guy does it regularly. That day he missed.

That was my first experience in the Super Bowl and it was weird. It's so heavily marketed and promoted, and people get caught up in all the glitz. It seems like there's more hype than game.

For us players, it goes by so fast. And all the hype and advertising for just one game. On top of that, there's a tremendous amount of money spent on tickets, hotel rooms, dining, and souvenirs. A lot of promotions were going on to get players' families and friends to the city for the game.

The only thing, I suppose, that makes it all feel worthwhile is when a team wins. We didn't win. If we had, perhaps I wouldn't remember all the negative aspects of that day.

We had reached the peak of our profession, and we had played in the year's biggest game. But it will go down in the history books that we lost. Few people will remember how or why we lost—everybody will read only that we lost.

◆ ❖ ◆

I frequently tell people that in life we will have sad days and we will have happy days. But joy, I point out, comes from the inside. Joy is one of God's greatest gifts to His children. Circumstances don't change a person's joy. I was sad we had lost so badly, but I had joy in the midst of disappointment. *I had actually played at the Super Bowl.*

"We can't let happiness or sadness control us," I said to one of my teammates. "There are bad things that happen throughout the world. But I can keep the joy inside because joy is a gift from God. If I'm determined to be joyful, nothing will take that away."

Chapter 23

THE RIGHT STRUCTURE

On March 6, 2006, I signed a contract with the Seahawks for the largest running-back deal in NFL history. I had waited, and God had answered. I've found that God truly blesses those who are willing to wait on Him. To tell you the truth, I received more money than I had expected or had ever prayed for.

So I left it with God. That was my part. The results are up to Him.

I don't need the money for myself. I want the money for what I can do to help others—as you'll see in this chapter. Money isn't a goal, it's a means to get to a goal. In this case, the goal is seeing lives changed.

But before I tell about that, I want to mention another dream I had. As you've already seen, God has used dreams on special occasions to guide me.

In February of 2003, I had one of those special dreams. I saw what looked like champagne glasses stacked in a pyramid-shaped structure. Over the pyramid hovered mystical-looking hands that held a bottle—and from the bottle, some kind of liquid was being poured. It was clear that as the liquid flowed into the top glass, it was supposed to overflow and filter downward and eventually fill all the glasses in the pyramid. That didn't happen.

The liquid poured into the top glass, but the glass tipped over and caused some of the others to crash. Several glasses broke, and the liquid spilled everywhere. Some of the glasses had a little in them from the accidental tipping-over—but most didn't.

I felt as if God was saying, *Shaun, I'm going to pour blessings on your life that will be unbelievable. However, if your structure isn't built on a strong foundation, the people at the bottom won't get blessed. There will be waste. Some will be blessed while others get pushed aside. It is possible for Me to pour blessings on you and for everything to flow in an orderly way to the bottom. Everybody can be filled. But for that to happen, your structure must be put together in the right way.*

After I told Valerie about the dream, I said, "I need to pay attention to everybody who works with us. My structure—my foundation—*has* to be right."

Let me explain how this has worked out. Part of my philosophy is that all of us need three types of people in our lives. In the early days of Christianity as recorded in the Bible, Paul was the teacher, Timothy the student, and Barnabas the encourager and what I might call the "accountability partner." All of us need these three roles filled in our lives, whether it's in business, family affairs, or spiritual matters. We all need a Paul, a Timothy, and a Barnabas. We can't build the right structure alone, though many people try.

Since that dream, Valerie and I have consistently prayed for a solid foundation and to have those three critical roles filled by trustworthy people. As a result, from time to time we've made changes in our organization…and we continually examine our lives to make sure *we're* still on track with God's plan for us. Valerie and I want to continue to hear and fully obey God's guidance. We have searched for the right mentors to advise us and for faithful workers to help fulfill the vision God has given me.

And God *has* guided us to the right people. Today I have business mentors like Erik Anderson of West River Capital and Gregg Alex, director of the Matt Talbot Center. I have football mentors like Stump Mitchell, Ricky Watters, and Tony Dorsett.

But the mentors I most want to mention are my spiritual mentors. My cousin Michael Story—who played such a key role in encouraging me toward marriage and during the NFL draft process—has taught me how to expect great things from God and how to respond when they happen. Another spiritual mentor is James Mitchell, who has taught me how to forgive. By his example, he showed me what a real man is and looks like. Ramon Diaz—who along with his wife, Suzanne, helped me sort out my relationship with Valerie—has taught me how to get to the root of who I am and who the Lord is. Roy Anderson has helped me learn to be a good communicator. From him, I also realized that true love involves sacrifice. My pastor, Casey Treat, has guided me to see that true faith in God happens after we have done all we can and have reached the end of our own resources. That's when we can still believe and call on Him.

I'm grateful for these men. They've helped me grasp the important things in life and have made me the man I am today. Being mentored by them has enabled me to see the powerful effect I can have in doing the same with others.

Because of my mentors' encouragement and help, I have a solid base for the structure God has given me. And one of the fruits of that solid structure is the Shaun Alexander Foundation (SAF), which empowers young men through education, athletics, character programs, and leadership training. We want to inspire kids to reach their full potential as mentors and then act as role models for the next generation. In short, *we mentor young men to change the world.*

Many young males today have not had good examples to show them how to become successful men. They want—and *need*—role models, and they're just not there. Their primary role models, of course, should have been their fathers, but too often the dads just didn't fulfill their roles. I call that the Great Curse—the Fatherless Plague.

When a dad doesn't step up to his responsibilities for his sons, those sons will often look to their peers as role models. But those peers usually have no direction themselves. How can they lead others into mature manhood when they're missing it themselves?

To combat this trend, I want to start the *new* trend I mentioned—seeing young men become positive role models and change the lives of those they influence. To do this, we try to get kids involved in organizations that will increase their vision for the future and help shape their faith. We want to help them get educated, not only to be successful, but to be future examples for the people and culture around them.

As part of that vision, SAF has partnered with three organizations: America's Foundation for Chess, The Choice Program, and the Fellowship of Christian Athletes.* Because I believe in these organizations and what they want to accomplish, I want you to know something about them too.

America's Foundation for Chess (AF4C) has the goal of providing elementary school students with opportunities to develop higher-level thinking skills, such as thinking ahead, making good choices, and thinking strategically. AF4C sponsors a program called First Move, which tries to bridge social, economic, and cultural boundaries in order to narrow and eventually close the achievement gap. The goal is to teach all second- and third-grade students across the country to play chess as part of classroom instruction, as described in this paragraph from their literature:

> The program is titled First Move™, and is comprised of three essential parts: The curriculum, training, and ongoing support. The program is taught in the classroom *during the school day*, once per week for an hour, and consists of 30 lessons over the course of the school year. The cost of the program is shared between the schools and AF4C. The key to the success of the program is preparing and training teachers to incorporate First Move™ into their classrooms. Our collaborative training program and "Teach the Teacher" workshops help connect the program to core subjects and learning concepts already being taught.

The mission of *The Choice Program* is to teach kids to stay in school and to make wise choices with their time and money. Their goal is to empower youth and to work with the families of those who need support services. The Choice Program works through schools to get students to set high goals and work toward meaningful participation and achieving their high expectations. As one young man who went through the program says, "My whole life was changed by one decision." Multiply that one young man by thousands, and you have a changed generation of young men.

The third organization I support is one I've already mentioned many times in these pages: *FCA—the Fellowship of Christian Athletes.* We've partnered

---

* Web sites for these organizations can be found at, respectively, **www.af4c.org; www.choices.org;** and **www.fca.org.**

with FCA to send hundreds of kids to camp each year. When I participate in these camps, the most outstanding thing I've seen is that top college and professional athletes stand before hundreds of kids and openly confess that they are Christians. They are among the best at what they do, and they credit Jesus Christ for giving them the ability to play as well as they do. Bobby Bowden said it best at one of the camps. He was repeating what he had heard one of the high school kids say: "I came to FCA camp to meet my gods—my sports idols—and then Coach Bowden told me about his God. And now today I take his God to be my God."

FCA's mission statement is to present to athletes and coaches and all whom they influence the challenge and adventure of receiving Jesus Christ as Savior and Lord, serving Him in their relationships, and in the fellowship of the church.

One other group I want to tell you about—my favorite—is *Club 37*. The idea for the group began when I was a student at the University of Alabama. Five of us would get together to encourage each other in our Christianity. Each week we would ask each other the following ten questions:

1. *Intimacy:* Have you spent daily time in the Scriptures and in prayer?
2. *Relationships:* How is your relationship with God? Are all of your relationships Christlike?
3. *Family:* Have you spent quality time with your family and friends?
4. *Love:* Have you blessed somebody or showed the love of Christ to anybody this week?
5. *Pride:* Have you told any half-truths or outright lies to put yourself in a better light to those around you?
6. *Purity:* Have you had any flirtations or lustful attitudes, tempting thoughts, or exposed yourself to any explicit materials that would not glorify God?

7. *Actions:* Have you taken anything that doesn't belong to you or said anything about or to anyone that would not be an example of Christ?

8. *Drugs:* Are you eating, drinking, or putting anything into your body that would not be Christlike?

9. *Focus:* Is there anything causing you to stumble or to stop you from keeping your focus on Christ?

10. *Honesty:* Have you lied on any of your answers today?

> What if every young man had a chance to be around buddies who would hold him accountable? The result would be strong men of faith—and a changed world.

We would try to be open with each other. At times we stumbled over the answer to a question. A few guys messed up on the same question two or three weeks in a row. When that happened, we simply reminded each other of this: *These questions are to help you stay on course with your decision to follow the Lord Jesus Christ and to help you see any flaws or weaknesses in your walk. That is the only goal.*

I realized that being part of that group helped me grow spiritually and become more fully committed. That's why I continue to use the same questions years later. I've learned that the best way to know where my heart is really at is to go through those questions regularly with a Barnabas, an accountability partner.

This realization led me to ask the question, "What if every young man had a chance to be around buddies who would hold him accountable?" The result would be strong men of faith—and a changed world. There is great strength to be found in accountability with a brother in Christ who loves you and is committed to seeing you grow.

As a result of this idea, Club 37 is now a national program that allows young men from every state, ages 14 to 24, to hold each other accountable for their own decisions to follow Jesus Christ.

Our goal is to get groups of three to five young men to meet once a week and go over the ten questions above. If we can get them to hold each other accountable within their own groups, they can be positive peers to each other.

My goal is to have 4000 young men in each state be members of Club 37.

When anyone asks me, "Is it possible?" I think to myself, *Was it possible that a poor kid from a small town in Kentucky could grow up with just a mother, go to a top university, graduate in just three and a half years, speak to youth all over the world and help lead thousands to Christ, become a professional football player, and win the MVP award?* The odds were against me, but I did it.

Club 37 has a goal; we intend to make the goal a reality.

Is it possible?

How do we know unless we try?

Chapter 24

ON THE SHOULDERS
OF GIANTS

*"If I have seen farther than others, it is because
I have stood on the shoulders of giants."*

I understand what Isaac Newton meant when he wrote those words.

It seems as if I've been able to do outstanding things...but that's only because I too have stood on the shoulders of giants. I've been surrounded by excellent people and gained much from them. My success is a result of knowing them.

Someone very wise once said, "Show me your friends, and I'll show you your future." I often quote this to others because I *believe* it.

Because of the friends and the giants in my life, I've learned two valuable lessons:

1. *Trials lead us to great things.* Too many people don't want to face the hardships that come with life, but if we want to reach the high levels in any phase of life, we *must* go through the tough times. I don't like hard times or adversity...but I admit that every difficulty that has come into my life has made me stronger.

   I believe that the heavy stones on our backs can become the stepping stones to get us to the next level. The struggles are preparation to make us what God wants us to become.

2. *God really does give us the desires of our hearts.* That's the key point of my life verse, Psalm 37:4.

I wouldn't want to end this book without saying more about the desires God has put in my heart. These desires drive me. They push me forward. They get me up in the morning, excited to see what God's next blessing will be. I can boil these desires down to two sentences.

First, *I want to make an impact for God's kingdom.* During my junior year in Alabama, Sam Collins, a teammate of mine, asked me to sign some T-shirts for his cousin. I started to write only my name.

"Why didn't you write your favorite Bible verse?" he asked. "Don't you think if you wrote it on there, everybody would eventually read it?"

I had never thought of that before. Since then, whenever I autograph anything I always add Psalm 37:4.

That same year—on August 30—I turned 21. It was that day that God gave me a platform to stand on to teach His Word. At Calvary Baptist Church, my church home during college, there's a church service where they invite the entire Alabama football team. It's called "Hello, 'Bama" and the church invites former players who are Christians to be the main speakers for that service.

Unlike many young men on their twenty-first birthdays, who celebrate by partying wild, I was one of the main speakers in that church service. My speaking that day has carried me into a higher calling of proclaiming God's Word.

And in March of 2003, I stepped up into an even higher calling. That month Pastor Casey Treat approached me and said, "Shaun, I feel it's time for you to be ordained."

His words floored me. I didn't know how to respond. I wasn't even quite sure what being "ordained" meant.

Pastor Treat explained that ordination was an acknowledgment of who I am, what I was already doing, and what I would continue to do in the future. We prayed together briefly, and I told him I'd pray more about being ordained.

And I did pray—a lot. At one point, I felt God ask me a tough question: *Are you ashamed of being ordained or of being associated with Me?*

I *wasn't* ashamed, and I knew the power of being obedient. I also trusted Casey. He is one of my spiritual mentors. If he felt I was ready to take such a step, I accepted that God was speaking through him and saying it was time for me to take a leap forward.

So on March 13, 2003, I was ordained. That night, Creflo Dollar, pastor of World Changers Church International in Atlanta, Georgia, preached. He said that people who don't work on their own character can be destroyed by their gifts: "Everybody was created especially for something…That is a gift, but if your character isn't strong enough to carry your gift, that gift will destroy you."

I listened intently to every word. His message challenged me to use both trials and victories as springboards to grow as a man, a student, a husband, and a teacher.

My second desire is, *I want to develop Timothys—the students of life—from all over the world.* That vision came from seeing the impact FCA camps had on some of the high school kids when I was a huddle leader. Some of those young men have gone forward for God and are being used by Him today. I know I'm not the only person who reached out to them, but I was given the opportunity to help them go in the right direction.

Here are two examples. First, when the film *The Passion of the Christ* came out, several of the Seahawks and I bought out a local theater for three special showings. That morning as I was praying, I felt God say to me, *You'll meet a new little brother today, and you're going to mentor him and teach him what to know.*

"All right, God," I prayed. "What does this boy look like?"

God didn't answer then, but I knew I'd find the boy.

At the end of the film, a pastor stood up and talked to those present who weren't believers. Several of us stood at the back, available to speak further to anyone who wanted to talk about the movie, God, or anything.

A young man named RaViel came up to me and started telling me about his cousin, Kellen. I was enjoying our conversation—and then it hit me. *I knew.*

"You're him!" I said.

RaViel probably thought I was crazy, but I knew this was the boy God had sent my way.

In the weeks following, RaViel and I got together regularly to talk about life, God, and the future. I taught him the value of knowing the Bible and making wise decisions in his life.

RaViel is now a sophomore in college. He loves God, and I believe that in the future he will become a great leader in whatever he undertakes.

The second example of a Timothy in my life is a young man named Jordan Shimon. He lives in a small town in Wisconsin. In April 2003, Valerie and I took a cruise from Florida to Cozumel, Mexico. Jordan was also on the ship, on spring break with his dad and little brother.

Val and I were on the deck one night and people were sitting around, talking, singing, and listening to music. We danced for a while. I noticed Jordan sitting and watching the grown-ups. I saw that he was the only teenager on the deck.

Here we are on this big boat, I thought, *and food is everywhere. There are all those arcades and dance areas downstairs, and high school girls are all around. Why is he here watching his dad dance?* After a few minutes, I turned to him and asked, "How old are you?"

"Sixteen," he answered.

"Why are you here on the deck and not downstairs with the high school kids playing video games and dancing and all that?"

"It's not my style," he said.

He was extremely tall, so I asked, "Do you play basketball?"

"Yeah, I play," he answered.

Our conversation ended, but I couldn't shake the feeling that there was something about Jordan…he had something about him I liked. I kept wondering if God wanted me to mentor him. "If I'm supposed to relate to this kid," I prayed, "then I'll see him tomorrow. I'll pull him to the side and talk to him."

The next day, while Val had a massage, I walked to the cafeteria. Just in front of me in line stood Jordan, his brother, and a couple of friends. We grabbed our food, and I invited the boys to eat with me.

They wanted to know about me, so I told them about my life, about who I was, and about a couple of the big games I had played in. As I answered, I had the sense Jordan wanted someone to tell him it was okay to be a man of God in today's world.

We connected that day, and Jordan became the newest Timothy in my life. That relationship still continues. At least once a month, I call him and give him Scriptures to read.

Right now I have about 30 Timothys in my life. I call them my little brothers, my mentees…and the future.

◆ ❖ ◆

At the time of this writing, I am 28 years old. Here's the most valuable truth I've learned in life: *I am a blessed man.*

I have been able to play professional football. I've gotten to know some of the spiritual giants of my generation, I've been able to hang with some of those who have made outstanding achievements, and I've been able to achieve some of the greatest honors—ones I never even thought about gaining.

I am blessed.

In high school I set a record of 350 yards and seven touchdowns in one game. In college, in my first-ever start, I scored five touchdowns. I became pro and won the MVP—and I played in the Super Bowl.

I am blessed.

I've spoken with Billy Graham, Franklin Graham, T.D. Jakes, Creflo Dollar, Casey Treat, Cece Winans, Third Day, Casting Crowns, the Katinas, DC Talk, Kirk Franklin, and Salvador.

I am blessed.

I've hung with Reggie White, Magic Johnson, Muhammad Ali, Barry Sanders, Buzz Cook, and Salome Thomas-EL.

I am blessed.

I've been on the cover of video games, been given the key to many cities—and in my home state of Kentucky I was given the Unbridled Spirit Award, an honor that's only been given out twice before. I've had a street named after me—I even had my own TV show for a while.

I have to laugh at how good God has been to me. I love that His Word is 100 percent right—He *does* give the desires of the heart to those who delight themselves in Him. So I end with this: Every night when I'm home, after I pray with my daughters and kiss my wife good night, I pause to thank God for giving me such a blessed life.

And many times, like a coach talking to his players, I've sensed God saying to me, *Shaun, this is only your first quarter...*

THE ROAD TO A
BLESSED LIFE

When I began this book I said I wanted my story to serve as an example of the goodness of God. I also said that part of my reason for writing *Touchdown Alexander* was to encourage readers to set goals for themselves—the higher the better. By thinking big and believing big, we'll *live* big.

Now, as I close the book, I'd like to offer some principles that have worked for me—principles I recommend for living a blessed life.

1. Put God first. God honors those who put Him first in their life. Not only does He honor them, but He *blesses* them. God *wants* to bless you. You don't have to beg for His blessing, you just have to put Him first and get in line with His way of living. The truth is that being a Christian—putting God first—is more than just talk. It takes all you've got to love Christ more than yourself. If you're not willing to love Him that much, I just say look out.

> Seek first his kingdom and his righteousness, and all these
> things will be given to you as well (Matthew 6:33-34).

2. Use trials to make you successful. When adversity comes our way—as it surely will—that's when we must lean hard on God's Word. At such times, we need to turn our eyes away from the adversity and get them on the sure promises of God.

The Word doesn't sustain us just in hard times—it guides us *all* the time. Make a habit of getting into the Word every day, even if only for a few minutes. Your heart and intimate relationship with God will grow the more time you spend in His Word. The Word will teach you how to live through tough times, and your trials will become steps to your next great victory. The result will be blessing in your life.

> Consider it pure joy, my brothers, whenever you face trials of many kinds, because you know that the testing of your faith develops perseverance. Perseverance must finish its work so that you may be mature and complete, not lacking anything (James 1:2-4).

3. Knowledge—chase it and use it. When it comes to a person living in sin, it usually happens for one of two reasons. Either the person has chosen Satan as their master, or they have been deceived and don't understand the seriousness of living in sin. Sin leads to death. Not having proper knowledge to make decisions in life can lead to destruction. Don't ever give up on learning. Chase knowledge and use it. It could save your life.

> My people are destroyed from lack of knowledge (Hosea 4:6).

4. Practice humility. Sometimes well-meaning people will try to puff you up. Make you think more of yourself than you ought. For me, one time that happened was the year I was franchised by the Seahawks. Many of my friends thought I deserved better and urged me to act on my own behalf. But Valerie and I had learned to wait on God in times like this. Waiting takes humility. Pride wants to rush in and get what we think we deserve. Scripture teaches that "pride goes before destruction." Pride also leads to embarrassment.

Learn to take the lower seat and let God promote you in His good time. The result is true blessing. Listen to what Jesus said about it:

When someone invites you to a wedding feast, do not take the place of honor, for a person more distinguished than you may have been invited. If so, the host who invited both of you will come and say to you, "Give this man your seat." Then, humiliated, you will have to take the least important place. But when you are invited, take the lowest place, so that when your host comes, he will say to you, "Friend, move up to a better place." Then you will be honored in the presence of all your fellow guests. For everyone who exalts himself will be humbled, and he who humbles himself will be exalted (Luke 14:8-11).

5. Be grateful and trust the Lord. When Durran and I were growing up in our small apartment on Shenandoah Drive in Florence, we didn't have much. But our mom made us feel like we had all we needed—and we did. Be grateful for what God has given you. Your talent…your money…your family…even if it seems like a little to you, when accepted with a grateful heart, God can multiply it. Trust God's plan for your life. Don't complain about what you don't have. Thank God for what you *do* have.

Trust in the LORD with all your heart
and lean not on your own understanding;
in all your ways acknowledge him,
and he will make your paths straight (Proverbs 3:5-6).

6. Discover your gift and step out. Everyone has been given talents that can be used to bring glory to God. And when we bring glory to God through the gifts He has given us, we are blessed. For me, the gift was athletic ability. As I stepped out and learned to use the gift God has given me, I've been blessed. *A very important key to blessing is finding your gifts and using them to the glory of God.*

Like I wrote at the beginning of the book, when I was a boy, I dreamed about being a successful businessman. None of my dreams centered around football. But when I became interested in peewee football because of Durran and my friend Ray, over the next several years I discovered that God's gifts to me were not what I thought they would be. And when I realized I could play football well—and this talent was a gift from God, and a way to achieve my dreams and also bring glory to Him—I stepped out and went after the prize of being a guy who made a lot of touchdowns.

Sometimes I wonder what my life would have been like if I had continued to say no to Durran and Ray's urging me to play football. Where would I be now? I don't know...but I do know that for me, finding football was the perfect will of God. I'm really glad I didn't miss it.

Do you know what your gifts are? Ask God to show you. Look around at the things in which you excel. Ask others who know you well what they think your gifts are. Then, go out and prosper with those gifts...as you follow God. See what doors He opens. In my case, God led me to some of the greatest football coaches in the sport. Under their leadership my abilities were sharpened, and records at all levels were broken.

My platform and my part on God's team were given to me by Him at birth. Your gift and part on God's team is already in you as well. Look for God to reveal your gifts—and then step out.

> There are different kinds of gifts, but the same Spirit. There are different kinds of service, but the same Lord. There are different kinds of working, but the same God works all of them in all men (1 Corinthians 12:4-6).

7. Be slow to judge and quick to forgive. I didn't realize that I was harboring bitterness toward my dad because he only seemed to be a part of my sports life and not part of my life off the football field. I was wrong to judge him without understanding why he was this way. When I found out his reasons, I was able to forgive him and get past the bitterness. Many talented people are unable to move forward because bitterness or some other negative emotion has gripped them. If you're holding a grudge, you may walk right past God's perfect will for you. Bitterness and unforgiveness can make us blind. Don't let that happen to you. Be a quick forgiver.

> Do not judge, and you will not be judged. Do not condemn, and you will not be condemned. Forgive, and you will be forgiven (Luke 6:37).

8. Know the will of God and be willing to wait on Him. We can't do the will of God unless we know it. We learn the will of God through knowing His Word and through allowing Him to lead us. And sometimes He leads us to *wait*. We don't like to wait. We want to move forward *now*. But if we know that God has a plan for us, we can afford to wait…and wait…and wait. And we can wait with confidence. His time is not our time.

For me, even a simple thing like waiting until the nineteenth pick of the first-round draft choices and hearing other players being selected before me, was hard—until I thought of my cousin Mike's reminder that God had everything under control. I had to *wait*. Later I had to wait through a full season as a franchised player, until the Seahawks offered me a contract that was well worth the wait.

The Bible is filled with the stories of men and women who waited for God—and some who didn't. Abraham and Sarah waited, but then they became impatient and tried to force God's hand. The result was Ishmael… and tragedy. Esau is an example of someone who was so impatient that he sold his birthright to Jacob for food. A lack of patience caused him to lose his blessing from God. The Hebrews traveling toward the Promised Land were impatient, and as result they were denied the very things they were so impatient for.

On the other hand, Hannah believed for a child from God…and waited. The early church waited in Jerusalem for the Holy Spirit to come. Even Jesus waited. His work didn't start until He was about 30 years old. Before that, He waited for God's timing.

Know the will of God and *wait*. It will come to pass.

> "I know the plans I have for you," declares the Lord, "plans to prosper you and not to harm you, plans to give you hope and a future" (Jeremiah 29:11).

> Wait for the Lord;
> be strong and take heart
> and wait for the Lord (Psalm 27:14).

9. Don't play games with your life. Recently Valerie was reading a book that brought up the point of how often we excuse sin in our lives. Most of us would never tell God point-blank that we don't love Him or don't care about what He did on the cross or don't care what His Word says about the way we choose to live. We just wouldn't do it.

Each of us really knows right from wrong. And we need to do the right and forsake the wrong. There's no gray area. Do the right thing…every time.

The Bible tells us that God judges the heart. That's because our heart will always follow its master. If the world is our master, then we will follow the world…and the fruit will be according to what the world offers. But if the Lord is the master of our heart, we will reap the fruit of blessing and bear His kind of fruit.

This business about playing games with God is why I often speak about what I call my "freak-out" verses. Here are some of them, all straight from Jesus' mouth. They're scriptures that should cause us to leave all the game-playing behind and have hearts solely for God.

> Enter through the narrow gate. For wide is the gate and broad is the road that leads to destruction, and many enter through it. But small is the gate and narrow the road that leads to life, and only a few find it (Matthew 7:13-14).

> Not everyone who says to me, "Lord, Lord," will enter the kingdom of heaven, but only he who does the will of my Father who is in heaven. Many will say to me on that day, "Lord, Lord, did we not prophesy in your name, and in your name drive out demons and perform many miracles?" Then I will tell them plainly, "I never knew you. Away from me, you evildoers!" (Matthew 7:21-23).

> These people honor me with their lips,
>   but their hearts are far from me.
> They worship me in vain;
>   their teachings are but rules taught by men (Matthew 15:8-9).

> If we deliberately keep on sinning after we have received the knowledge of the truth, no sacrifice for sins is left, but only a fearful expectation of judgment and of raging fire that will consume the enemies of God (Hebrews 10:26-27).

To sum up these four Scriptures, I say this: The road to heaven is narrow. Many people will live religiously for God instead of entering into a relationship with Him. They may say all the right things, but behind closed doors, their hearts are not for Jesus. They will deliberately sin, which shows their true heart. We all sin daily, but to *deliberately* sin is to show that you don't really love God or honor what Jesus did on the cross.

10. Leave the results to God. For every person, there's our part and there's God's part. When we do our part, we can rest easy that God will do His part. When Valerie and I bought a house following the leading of God, we still didn't know if we'd be staying in Seattle. We had to come to the place where we said to God, "We'd like to stay here and serve you in Seattle...*but* we're willing to move where you want us. God, *You* choose where You want us."

And then we left the results to God. The result was that we had peaceful hearts. We no longer were holding on to what *we* wanted to do. And God did what He wanted...and in so doing, He fulfilled the desires of my heart. When you go after God, His desires become your desires.

It all comes back to this:

> Delight yourself in the LORD
> and he will give you the desires of your heart (Psalm 37:4).

If you stay in this order you won't be able to stop God's blessings from coming to your life. Live holy and righteous every day. No matter what others do.

May your life be *truly* blessed.

STATS AND YEAR-BY-YEAR HIGHLIGHTS

SHAUN ALEXANDER'S CAREER AT THE UNIVERSITY OF ALABAMA

1996–1999 Stats

Year	G	Rush	Yds	TD	Avg	Long	Rec	Yds	Avg	TD
1996	11	77	589	6	7.6	73	7	53	7.6	0
1997	9	90	415	3	4.6	27	4	37	9.3	0
1998	11	258	1178	13	4.6	44	26	385	14.8	4
1999	11	302	1383	19	4.6	38	25	303	13.4	4
Total	42	727	3565	41	4.9	N.A.	62	778	13.0	8

Shaun's Alabama Career Bests

†Most touchdowns/game	5 (vs. BYU): 1998
†Most touchdowns/season	24 (19 rush, 4 receiving, 1 KOR). 1999
Touchdowns/career	50 (41 rush, 8 receiving, 1 KOR): 1996–1999
†Most yards rushing/game	291 (vs. LSU, 20 atts): 1999
Most yards rushing/season	1383 (302 atts): 1999
†Yards rushing/career	3565 (727 atts): 1996–1999
Most rushes/game	36 (vs. Ole Miss, 1999; vs. Southern Mississippi, 1998)
†Most rushes/season	302 (1383 yards): 1999
†Rushes/career	727 (3565 yards): 1996–1999
†Average gain per rush/game	14.6 (vs. LSU, 291 yards on 20 atts): 1996
†Most rushing touchdowns/season	19 (1999)
†Rushing touchdowns/career	41 (1996–1999)

KOR = kickoff return
† Alabama School Records

SHAUN ALEXANDER'S
NFL CAREER STATISTICS

Rushing

Year	Team	G	GS	Att	Yards	Avg	Lg	TD
2000	Seattle Seahawks	16	1	64	313	4.9	50	2
2001	Seattle Seahawks	16	12	309	1318	4.3	88	14
2002	Seattle Seahawks	16	16	295	1175	4.0	58	16
2003	Seattle Seahawks	16	15	326	1435	4.4	55	14
2004	Seattle Seahawks	16	16	353	1696	4.8	44	16
2005	Seattle Seahawks	16	16	370	1880	5.1	88	27
Total		**96**	**76**	**1717**	**7817**	**4.6**	**88**	**89**

Receiving

Year	Team	G	GS	No	Yards	Avg	Lg	TD	20+
2000	Seattle Seahawks	16	1	5	41	8.2	18	0	0
2001	Seattle Seahawks	16	12	44	343	7.8	28	2	2
2002	Seattle Seahawks	16	16	59	460	7.8	80	2	1
2003	Seattle Seahawks	16	15	42	295	7.0	22	2	3
2004	Seattle Seahawks	16	16	23	170	7.4	24	4	1
2005	Seattle Seahawks	16	16	15	78	5.2	9	1	0
Total		**96**	**76**	**188**	**1387**	**7.4**	**80**	**11**	**7**

SHAUN ALEXANDER'S
COLLEGE CAREER HIGHLIGHTS

- Alabama's all-time rushing leader, with 3565 yards (4.9 average) in four seasons—breaking Bobby Humphrey's school mark of 3420 yards established from 1985–1988.

- Set school records with 727 rushing attempts, 15 100-yard games, 41 rushing touchdowns, and 50 total touchdowns.

- Overall, he held 15 school records and three Southeastern Conference (SEC) marks when he left the Crimson Tide.

- He was voted SEC Offensive Player of the Year for 1999—his senior year—by the coaches.

- As a senior, he averaged 125.73 yards per game.

- His 19 touchdowns during his senior year established a conference record.

- Reached 1000 yards on the ground in the seventh game of his senior year—the fastest of any 'Bama player.

- Finished his college career with 161 yards on 25 carries, with three touchdowns, playing Michigan in the Orange Bowl.

- Selected for the 1999 Coaches' All-America Team.

SHAUN ALEXANDER'S
PROFESSIONAL CAREER HIGHLIGHTS

2000 Highlights

- Saw action in all 16 games and started one game in a reserve role during his rookie season.

- Finished the season second on the team, behind Ricky Watters, rushing 64 times for 313 yards.

- His 4.9-yard average ranked second among rookie running backs during that NFL season.

- Earned his first career start in a split backfield with Watters at Kansas City (10/02) and turned in his finest performance of the season. He rushed for season highs with 11 carries and 74 yards, which included 55 yards on six carries on a touchdown drive just before halftime to give Seattle a 14–7 lead—a drive he capped with his first career touchdown run, from 7 yards out.

2001 Highlights

- Despite starting only 12 games, rushed for 1318 yards on 309 attempts—the fifth-highest rushing total in team history—while becoming just the fourth back to eclipse the 1000-yard mark, joining Curt Warner, Chris Warren, and Ricky Watters.
- Led the NFL with 14 rushing touchdowns, just one shy of Chris Warren's 1995 team record.
- Ranked third in the AFC (sixth in the NFL), with 1661 total yards from scrimmage, and ranked sixth in the AFC with 76 first downs.
- Versus Jacksonville (10/7) rushed 31 times for 176 yards and two touchdowns while earning his first AFC Offensive Player of the Week award.
- Earned second AFC Offensive Player of the Week award after one of the best games in NFL history versus the Oakland Raiders (11/11), rushing for a franchise-record 266 yards on 35 carries with three touchdowns. Performance was the fourth-highest total in NFL.

2002 Highlights

- Started all 16 games at running back en route to rushing for an NFC-leading (second-highest in NFL) and franchise-record 16 touchdowns, eclipsing his own mark of 15 from 2001.*
- Also led the NFC (second in the NFL) and set a team record with 18 combined touchdowns and in non-kicker scoring with 108 points.
- Rushed for 1175 yards on 295 carries (4.0 average).
- Finished second in the NFC with 80 first downs.
- Had a career-high 59 receptions (third among NFC running backs) for 460 yards.

---

* The Seahawks moved to the NFC as of the 2002 season.

- Versus Minnesota (9/29), rushed for 139 yards on 24 carries, scoring a career-high and franchise-record five touchdowns. All scores were in the first half to set an NFL record for most touchdowns in one half. Five touchdowns were also the second most in NFL history, tying him with nine others.

- Totaled a season-high 145 yards versus Kansas City (11/24) with two touchdowns.

2003 Highlights

- After rushing for a career high 1435 yards and 16 touchdowns (two shy of his own team record of 18 in 2002), earned his first trip to the Pro Bowl.

- After starting 34 straight games, missed start against St. Louis after helping deliver his first child, daughter Heaven.

- Had 14 rushing scores, which was second in the NFC and moved him into third overall for the Seahawks, with 52 career touchdowns.

- Had seven games in which he rushed for more than 100 yards and three multiple touchdown games (13 for his career).

2004 Highlights

- Earned second trip to Pro Bowl after leading the NFL with a career-high and Seahawks-record 20 total touchdowns (16 rushing, career-high 4 receiving) and 120 points scored.

- Finished first in the NFC (second in the NFL) with 16 rushing touchdowns. Led the NFC (and was second in the NFL) with a career-high and Seahawks record of 1696 yards rushing (4.8 rushing average).

- With rushing touchdown versus Miami (11/21), passed Curt Warner to become Seattle's all-time leader in rushing touchdowns. His 154 rushing yards versus Arizona (12/26) passed Chris Warren's single-season rushing record (1545 yards).

- Versus Carolina (10/31), toted the ball for 30-plus times for the fourth time in career, racking up 32 carries for season-high 195 yards and a touchdown.
- Versus Arizona (12/26), scored sixteenth rushing touchdown, tying his Seahawks record (2002); 19 carries gave him 353 on the season, also a Seahawks single-season record.

2005 Highlights

- Won the NFL rushing title, along with the season touchdown record for running backs, and was named league MVP.
- Broke franchise record for the most rushing yards in Seattle Seahawks history.
- Became the first running back in NFL history to record 15 or more touchdowns in five consecutive seasons and the first player to score 19 rushing or receiving TDs in only ten games.
- Became the first Seahawks player to appear on the cover of Sports Illustrated, with the headline "Do you know his name?" In a fitting piece of irony, the article failed to spell his name correctly (*Sean* instead of *Shaun*).
- On January 1, 2006, versus the Green Bay Packers, set the record for touchdowns in a season—28.
- Also won his first NFL rushing title with 1880 yards. Joined Emmitt Smith, Priest Holmes, and Marshall Faulk as the only running backs to record consecutive seasons of 20 or more touchdowns.
- Four days later, on January 5, was named 2005 NFL MVP with 19 out of 50 votes. Was named Associated Press Offensive Player of the Year the next day, receiving 34 votes of a panel of 50 NFL sportswriters and broadcasters.